Unity AI Game Programming
Second Edition

Leverage the power of Unity 5 to create stunningly life-like AI entities in your games!

Ray Barrera

Aung Sithu Kyaw

Clifford Peters

Thet Naing Swe

PUBLISHING

BIRMINGHAM - MUMBAI

Unity AI Game Programming
Second Edition

First published: July 2013

Second edition: September 2015

Production reference: 1180915

Published by Packt Publishing Ltd.
Livery Place
35 Livery Street
Birmingham B3 2PB, UK.

ISBN 978-1-78528-827-2

www.packtpub.com

Credits

About the Authors

Ray Barrera was a tinker in his childhood. From making mods and custom maps in games such as *StarCraft* and *Unreal Tournament* to developing open source role-playing games using RPG Maker, he always had a passion for game development. The passion stayed with him, and after many years as a hobbyist, he decided to take the plunge into professional development.

In the initial stages of his career, he was fortunate enough to work on educational and research projects for major contractors in the defense industry, allowing him to blend his love for games with his innate desire to teach and create interactive experiences. Since then, he has straddled the line between entertainment and education. Unity was the logical weapon of choice for him as it gave him the flexibility to create games and applications and iterate quickly. From being an original member of the Los Angeles Unity meetup to helping coordinate Unity workshops at local colleges and high schools, he has been very active in the Unity community. You can follow him on Twitter at `@ray_barrera`.

There are too many people to name, but I'd like to thank the team at Packt Publishing for this exciting opportunity, and of course, my wonderful friends and family, especially my parents, who always encouraged me to follow my passion and supported me along every step of the way. I'd also like to thank the Twistory team for being such an amazing group of people—Danny, JP, DW, Richard, the lovely "Purple", and everyone else—whom I was so fortunate to work with. Thanks to Peter Trennum for the mentorship and leadership he has provided at this stage in my career. Lastly, I'd like to thank Gianni, my brother, for all the love and support over the years.

Aung Sithu Kyaw has been in the technical industry for over a decade. He is passionate about graphics programming, creating video games, writing, and sharing knowledge with others. He holds an MSc in digital media technology from the Nanyang Technological University (NTU), Singapore. Over the last few years, he has worked in various positions, including research programmer and senior game programmer. Lastly, he worked as a research associate, which involved implementing a sensor-based real-time movie system using Unreal Development Kit. In 2011, he founded a tech start-up, which focuses on interactive media productions and backend server-side technologies. He is currently based in Myanmar and working on his latest company's product, a gamified social opinion network for Myanmar.

He can be followed on Twitter at `@aungsithu` and LinkedIn at `http://linkedin.com/in/aungsithu`.

Thanks to my coauthors who worked really hard with me on this book despite their busy schedules and helped get this book published. Thanks also goes to the team at Packt Publishing for having us produce this book. And finally, thanks to the awesome guys at Unity3D for building this amazing toolset and making it affordable to indie game developers. Dedicated to L!

Clifford Peters is a programmer and a computer scientist. He was the technical reviewer for *Unity Game Development Essentials, Unity 3D Game Development by Example Beginner's Guide, Unity 3 Game Development HOTSHOT, Unity 3.x Game Development by Example Beginner's Guide, Unity iOS Game Development Beginner's Guide*, and *Unity iOS Essentials*, all by Packt Publishing.

Thet Naing Swe is the founder and CTO of Joy Dash Pte Ltd, based in Singapore. He graduated from the University of Central Lancashire with a major in game design and development and started his career as a game programmer at one of the UK-based Nintendo DS game development studios. In 2010, he relocated to Singapore and worked as a graphics programmer at the Nanyang Technological University (NTU) on a cinematic research project.

At Joy Dash, he's responsible for interactive digital media consulting projects, especially in education, casual games, and augmented reality projects using Unity 3D as the main development tool. He can be reached via thetnswe@gmail.com.

I would like to thank the whole team at Packt Publishing for keeping track of all the logistics and making sure the book was published no matter what; I really appreciate this. I'd also like to thank my parents for supporting me all these years and letting me pursue my dream of becoming a game developer. Without all your support, I wouldn't be here today.

And finally, a huge thanks to my wife, May Thandar Aung, for allowing me to work on this book after office hours, late at night, and even on weekends. Without your understanding and support, this book would have been delayed for another year. I'm grateful to have your support in whatever I do. I love you.

About the Reviewers

Mohammedun Bakir Bagasrawala is a Unity AI engineer at Beachhead Studio, an Activision Blizzard studio. He holds a master's degree in computer science with a specialization in game development from the University of Southern California. He worked at DreamWorks Animation, where he was part of the team that built innovative AI technologies. He then moved to Treyarch and had the utmost pleasure of working on *Call of Duty: Black Ops 3*, implementing several features of this game. Apart from his professional experience, he has also been an AI lead across a gamut of mobile, console, and board games at the USC GamePipe Laboratory.

I would like to thank my parents, Shabbir and Rita; my siblings, Esmail and Jacklyn; and my best friend, Afreen, for helping me become who I am today. I would also like to thank Giselle, Pratik, Rushabh, Neel, Soham, Kashyap, Sabarish, and Alberto as they have stood by me throughout. Lastly, I would like to thank my former managers, Mark, Vishwa, Ryan, and Trevor and my professors, Artem and Michael Zyda.

Adam Boyce is a software developer and an independent game developer who specializes in C# scripting, game design, and AI development. His experience includes application support, software development, and data architecture with various Canadian corporations. He was also the technical reviewer for *Unity AI Programming Essentials, Packt Publishing*. You can read his development blog at www.gameovertures.ca and follow him on Twitter at https://twitter.com/AdamBoyce4.

I'd like to thank my wife, Gail, for supporting me throughout the review process and also in my life and career.

Jack Donovan is a game developer and software engineer who has been working with the Unity3D engine since its third major release. He studied at Champlain College in Burlington, Vermont, where he received a BS in game programming.

He currently works at IrisVR, a virtual reality start-up in New York City, and develops software that allows architects to generate virtual reality experiences from their CAD models or blueprints. Prior to this company, he worked as part of a small independent game team with fellow students, and that was when he wrote *OUYA Game Development by Example Beginner's Guide, Packt Publishing*.

Chaima Jemmali holds an engineering degree in networks and telecommunication. Currently, she is a Fulbright scholar, pursuing a master's degree in interactive media and game development at the Worcester Polytechnic Institute, Worcester, Massachusetts.

She has always wanted to share her love for programming through her master's project, which is a serious game that teaches coding, her internship as an instructor with iD Tech Camps, and by contributing to the success of this book.

I would like to thank the writers and everyone who worked hard to help produce this book.

Akshay Sunil Masare is currently a student at the Indian Institute of Technology, Kanpur, working toward his BTech in computer science and engineering. He has developed various games on Android and also on the Web. He has also worked on an AI agent that uses deep learning and convolutional neural networks to learn and train itself to play any game on the Atari 2600 platform.

www.PacktPub.com

Support files, eBooks, discount offers, and more

For support files and downloads related to your book, please visit www.PacktPub.com.

Did you know that Packt offers eBook versions of every book published, with PDF and ePub files available? You can upgrade to the eBook version at www.PacktPub.com and as a print book customer, you are entitled to a discount on the eBook copy. Get in touch with us at service@packtpub.com for more details.

At www.PacktPub.com, you can also read a collection of free technical articles, sign up for a range of free newsletters and receive exclusive discounts and offers on Packt books and eBooks.

https://www2.packtpub.com/books/subscription/packtlib

Do you need instant solutions to your IT questions? PacktLib is Packt's online digital book library. Here, you can search, access, and read Packt's entire library of books.

Why subscribe?

- Fully searchable across every book published by Packt
- Copy and paste, print, and bookmark content
- On demand and accessible via a web browser

Free access for Packt account holders

If you have an account with Packt at www.PacktPub.com, you can use this to access PacktLib today and view 9 entirely free books. Simply use your login credentials for immediate access.

Table of Contents

Preface

In this book, we'll be exploring the world of artificial intelligence (AI) as it relates to game development. No matter what kind of game you are developing, you will surely find a myriad of uses for the content in this book—perhaps in ways that even I could not imagine.

The goal of this book is not to make you an expert, as it would take many, many, years and many more pages to do this, but to provide you with the knowledge and tools to embark on your own AI journey. This book covers the essentials, and by the end, you will have all that you need to implement AI in your own game, whether you choose to expand upon the examples provided or take the knowledge and do something new and exciting with it.

You will get the most out of this book and the examples provided by following along and tinkering with the code and project files provided. Each chapter will provide a conceptual background and some examples and will challenge readers to think of ways in which they can use these concepts in their games.

What this book covers

Chapter 1, The Basics of AI in Games, aims to demystify some of the most basic concepts of AI as it is a very vast and intimidating topic.

Chapter 2, Finite State Machines and You, covers one of the most widely used concepts in AI—the finite state machine.

Chapter 3, Implementing Sensors, covers some of the most important ways for a game AI agent to perceive the world around it. The realism of an AI agent is directly linked to how it responds to its environment.

Chapter 4, Finding Your Way, covers the most widely used pattern in pathfinding for game AI agents. The agents in games need to traverse the areas of the game levels and maneuver around obstacles along the way.

Chapter 5, Flocks and Crowds, covers flocking and crowd simulation algorithms, allowing you to handle the unison movements of the agents in your game rather than having to figure out the logic for each agent.

Chapter 6, Behavior Trees, covers the process of implementing a custom behavior tree as it is one of the most common ways to implement complex and compound AI behaviors in games.

Chapter 7, Using Fuzzy Logic to Make Your AI Seem Alive, shows you how to let the game AI agents make decisions based on various factors in a non-binary way. Fuzzy logic mimics the way humans make decisions.

Chapter 8, How It All Comes Together, covers an example of how various systems come together in a single-objective game template that can be easily expanded upon.

What you need for this book

To use the sample content provided with this book, you'll need a copy of Unity 5, which you can download for free from `https://unity3d.com/get-unity`. The system requirements for Unity can be found at `https://unity3d.com/get-unity`.

MonoDevelop, the IDE that comes bundled with Unity 5, is suggested but not required for this book as any text editor will do just fine. However, MonoDevelop comes with everything you need to write and debug code out of the box, including autocompletion, without the need for plugins or extensions.

Who this book is for

This book is intended for Unity developers with a basic understanding of C# and the Unity editor. Whether you're looking to build your first game or trying to expand your knowledge as a game programmer, you will find plenty of exciting information and examples of game AI in terms of concepts and implementation. This book does not require any prior technical knowledge of how game AI works.

Conventions

In this book, you will find a number of text styles that distinguish between different kinds of information. Here are some examples of these styles and an explanation of their meaning.

Code words in text, database table names, folder names, filenames, file extensions, pathnames, dummy URLs, user input, and Twitter handles are shown as follows: "We'll name it `TankFsm`."

A block of code is set as follows:

```
using UnityEngine;
using System.Collections;

public class TankPatrolState : StateMachineBehaviour {

    // OnStateEnter is called when a transition starts and the state
machine starts to evaluate this state
    //override public void OnStateEnter(Animator animator,
AnimatorStateInfo stateInfo, int layerIndex) {
    //
    //}

    // OnStateUpdate is called on each Update frame between
OnStateEnter and OnStateExit callbacks
    //override public void OnStateUpdate(Animator animator,
AnimatorStateInfo stateInfo, int layerIndex) {
    //
    //}

    // OnStateExit is called when a transition ends and the state
machine finishes evaluating this state
    //override public void OnStateExit(Animator animator,
AnimatorStateInfo stateInfo, int layerIndex) {
    //
    //}

    // OnStateMove is called right after Animator.OnAnimatorMove().
Code that processes and affects root motion should be implemented here
    //override public void OnStateMove(Animator animator,
AnimatorStateInfo stateInfo, int layerIndex) {
    //
    //}
```

```
    // OnStateIK is called right after Animator.OnAnimatorIK(). Code
that sets up animation IK (inverse kinematics) should be implemented
here.
    //override public void OnStateIK(Animator animator,
AnimatorStateInfo stateInfo, int layerIndex) {
    //
    //}
}
```

New terms and **important words** are shown in bold. Words that you see on the screen, for example, in menus or dialog boxes, appear in the text like this: "When the panels are closed, you can still create new layers by clicking on the **Layers** dropdown and selecting **Create New Layer**."

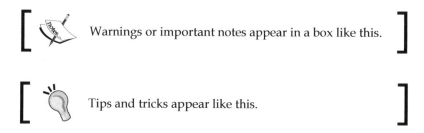

Warnings or important notes appear in a box like this.

Tips and tricks appear like this.

Reader feedback

Feedback from our readers is always welcome. Let us know what you think about this book—what you liked or disliked. Reader feedback is important for us as it helps us develop titles that you will really get the most out of.

To send us general feedback, simply e-mail feedback@packtpub.com, and mention the book's title in the subject of your message.

If there is a topic that you have expertise in and you are interested in either writing or contributing to a book, see our author guide at www.packtpub.com/authors.

Customer support

Now that you are the proud owner of a Packt book, we have a number of things to help you to get the most from your purchase.

Downloading the example code

You can download the example code files from your account at http://www. packtpub.com for all the Packt Publishing books you have purchased. If you purchased this book elsewhere, you can visit https://www.packtpub.com/support and register to have the files e-mailed directly to you.

Downloading the color images of this book

We also provide you with a PDF file that has color images of the screenshots/diagrams used in this book. The color images will help you better understand the changes in the output. You can download this file from https://www.packtpub.com/sites/default/files/downloads/8272OT_ColorImages.pdf.

Errata

Although we have taken every care to ensure the accuracy of our content, mistakes do happen. If you find a mistake in one of our books—maybe a mistake in the text or the code—we would be grateful if you could report this to us. By doing so, you can save other readers from frustration and help us improve subsequent versions of this book. If you find any errata, please report them by visiting http://www.packtpub.com/submit-errata, selecting your book, clicking on the **Errata Submission Form** link, and entering the details of your errata. Once your errata are verified, your submission will be accepted and the errata will be uploaded to our website or added to any list of existing errata under the Errata section of that title.

To view the previously submitted errata, go to https://www.packtpub.com/books/content/support and enter the name of the book in the search field. The required information will appear under the **Errata** section.

Piracy

Piracy of copyrighted material on the Internet is an ongoing problem across all media. At Packt, we take the protection of our copyright and licenses very seriously. If you come across any illegal copies of our works in any form on the Internet, please provide us with the location address or website name immediately so that we can pursue a remedy.

Please contact us at copyright@packtpub.com with a link to the suspected pirated material.

We appreciate your help in protecting our authors and our ability to bring you valuable content.

Questions

If you have a problem with any aspect of this book, you can contact us at questions@packtpub.com, and we will do our best to address the problem.

1
The Basics of AI in Games

Artificial Intelligence (AI), in general, is a vast, deep, and intimidating topic. The uses for it are diverse, ranging from robotics, to statistics, to (more relevantly to us) entertainment, and more specifically, video games. Our goal will be to demystify the subject by breaking down the use of AI into relatable, applicable solutions, and to provide accessible examples that illustrate the concepts in the ways that cut through the noise and go straight for the core ideas.

This chapter will give you a little background on AI in academics, traditional domains, and game-specific applications. Here are the topics we'll cover:

- Exploring how the application and implementation of AI in games is different from other domains
- Looking at the special requirements for AI in games
- Looking at the basic AI patterns used in games

This chapter will serve as a reference for later chapters, where we'll implement the AI patterns in Unity.

Creating the illusion of life

Living organisms such as animals and humans have some sort of intelligence that helps us in making a particular decision to perform something. Our brains respond to stimuli, albeit through sound, touch, smell, or vision, and then convert that data into information that we can process. On the other hand, computers are just electronic devices that can accept binary data, perform logical and mathematical operations at high speed, and output the results. So, AI is essentially the subject of making computers appear to be able to think and decide like living organisms to perform specific operations.

AI and its many related studies are dense and vast, but it is really important to understand the basics of AI being used in different domains before digging deeper into the subject. AI is just a general term; its implementations and applications are different for different purposes, solving different sets of problems.

Before we move on to game-specific techniques, we'll take a look at the following research areas in AI applications that have advanced tremendously over the last decade. Things that used to be considered science fiction are quickly becoming science fact, such as autonomous robots. You need not look very far to find a great example of AI advances—your smart phone most likely has a digital assistant feature that relies on some new AI-related technology. Here are some of the research fields driving AI:

- **Computer vision**: It is the ability to take visual input from sources such as videos and cameras and analyze them to do particular operations such as facial recognition, object recognition, and optical-character recognition.

- **Natural language processing (NLP)**: It is the ability that allows a machine to read and understand the languages as we normally write and speak. The problem is that the languages we use today are difficult for machines to understand. There are many different ways to say the same thing, and the same sentence can have different meanings according to the context. NLP is an important step for machines since they need to understand the languages and expressions we use, before they can process them and respond accordingly. Fortunately, there's an enormous amount of data sets available on the Web that can help researchers to do the automatic analysis of a language.

- **Common sense reasoning**: This is a technique that our brains can easily use to draw answers even from the domains we don't fully understand. Common sense knowledge is a usual and common way for us to attempt certain questions since our brains can mix and interplay between the context, background knowledge, and language proficiency. But making machines to apply such knowledge is very complex and still a major challenge for researchers.

- **Machine learning**: This may sound like something straight out of a science fiction movie, and the reality is not too far off. Computer programs generally consist of a static set of instructions, which take input and provide output. Machine learning focuses on the science of writing algorithms and programs that can learn from the data processed by said program.

Leveling up your game with AI

AI in games dates back all the way to the earliest games, even as far back as Namco's arcade hit Pac-Man. The AI was rudimentary at best, but even in Pac-Man, each of the enemies, Blinky, Pinky, Inky, and Clyde had unique behaviors that challenged the player in different ways. Learning those behaviors and reacting to them added a huge amount of depth to the game that keeps players coming back, even after over 30 years since its release.

It's the job of a good game designer to make the game challenging enough to be engaging, but not so difficult that a player can never win. To this end, AI is a fantastic tool that can help abstract the patterns that entities in games follow to make them seem more organic, alive, and real. Much like an animator through each frame or an artist through his brush, a designer or programmer can breathe life into their creations by a clever use of the AI techniques covered in this book.

The role of AI in games is to make it fun by providing challenging entities to compete with and interesting **non-player characters** (**NPCs**) that behave realistically inside the game world. The objective here is not to replicate the whole thought process of humans or animals, but merely to sell the illusion of life and make NPCs seem intelligent by reacting to the changing situations inside the game world in a way that makes sense to the player.

Technology allows us to design and create intricate patterns and behaviors, but we're not yet at the point where AI in games even begins to resemble true human behavior. While smaller, more powerful chips, buckets of memory, and even distributed computing have given programmers a much higher computational ceiling to dedicate to AI, at the end of the day, resources are still shared between other operations such as graphic rendering, physics simulation, audio processing, animation, and others, all in real time. All these systems have to play nice with each other to achieve a steady frame rate throughout the game. Like all the other disciplines in game development, optimizing AI calculations remains a huge challenge for the AI developers.

Using AI in Unity

In this section, we'll walk through some of the AI techniques being used in different types of games. We'll learn how to implement each of these features in Unity in the upcoming chapters. Unity is a flexible engine that affords us a number of avenues to implement AI patterns. Some are ready to go out of the box, so to speak, while we'll have to build others from scratch. In this book, we'll focus on implementing the most essential AI patterns within Unity so that you can get your game's AI entities up and running quickly. Learning and implementing these techniques with this book will serve as a fundamental first step into the vast world of AI.

Defining the agent

Before jumping into our first technique, we should be clear on a key term you'll see used throughout the book—the agent. An agent, as it relates to AI, is our artificially intelligent entity. When we talk about our AI, we're not specifically referring to a character, but an entity that displays complex behavior patterns, which we can refer to as non-random or in other words, intelligent. This entity can be a character, creature, vehicle, or anything else. The agent is the autonomous entity, executing the patterns and behaviors we'll be covering. With that out of the way, let's jump in.

Finite State Machines

Finite State Machines (FSM) can be considered as one of the simplest AI models, and they are commonly used in games. A state machine basically consists of a set number of states that are connected in a graph by the transitions between them. A game entity starts with an initial state and then looks out for the events and rules that will trigger a transition to another state. A game entity can only be in exactly one state at any given time.

For example, let's take a look at an AI guard character in a typical shooting game. Its states could be as simple as patrolling, chasing, and shooting:

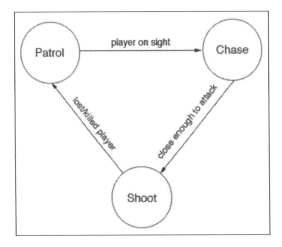

There are basically four components in a simple FSM:

- **States**: This component defines a set of distinct states that a game entity or an NPC can choose from (patrol, chase, and shoot)
- **Transitions**: This component defines relations between different states
- **Rules**: This component is used to trigger a state transition (player on sight, close enough to attack, and lost/killed player)
- **Events**: This is the component that will trigger to check the rules (guard's visible area, distance with the player, and so on)

FSMs are a commonly used go-to AI pattern in game development because they are relatively easy to implement, visualize, and understand. Using simple if/else statements or switch statements, we can easily implement an FSM. It can get messy as we start to have more states and more transitions. We'll look at how to manage a simple FSM more in depth in *Chapter 2, Finite State Machines and You*.

Seeing the world through our agent's eyes

In order to make our AI convincing, our agent needs to be able to respond to events around him, the environment, the player, and even other agents. Much like real-living organisms, our agent can rely on sight, sound, and other "physical" stimuli. However, we have the advantage of being able to access much more data within our game than a real organism can from their surroundings, such as the player's location, regardless of whether or not they are in the vicinity, their inventory, the location of items around the world, and any variable you chose to expose to that agent in your code.

In the following image, our agent's field of vision is represented by the cone in front of it, and its hearing range is represented by the grey circle surrounding it:

Vision, sound, and other senses can be thought of, at their most essential level, as data. Vision is just light particles, sound is just vibrations, and so on. While we don't need to replicate the complexity of a constant stream of light particles bouncing around and entering our agent's eyes, we can still model the data in a way that produces similar results.

As you might imagine, we can similarly model other sensory systems, and not just the ones used for biological beings such as sight, sound, or smell, but even digital and mechanical systems that can be used by enemy robots or towers, for example, sonar and radar.

Path following and steering

Sometimes, we want our AI characters to roam around in the game world, following a roughly-guided or thoroughly-defined path. For example, in a racing game, the AI opponents need to navigate on the road. In an RTS game, your units need to be able to get from wherever they are to the location you tell them to, navigating through the terrain, and around each other.

To appear intelligent, our agents need to be able to determine where they are going, and if they can reach that point, they should be able to route the most efficient path and modify that path if an obstacle appears as they navigate. As you'll learn in later chapters, even path following and steering can be represented via a finite state machine. You will then see how these systems begin to tie in.

In this book, we will cover the primary methods of pathfinding and navigation, starting with our own implementation of an A* Pathfinding system, followed by an overview of Unity's built-in **navigation mesh (NavMesh)** feature.

Using A* Pathfinding

There are many games where you can find monsters or enemies that follow the player, or go to a particular point while avoiding obstacles. For example, let's take a look at a typical RTS game. You can select a group of units and click on a location where you want them to move or click on the enemy units to attack them. Your units then need to find a way to reach the goal without colliding with the obstacles. The enemy units also need to be able to do the same. Obstacles could be different for different units. For example, an air force unit might be able to pass over a mountain, while the ground or artillery units need to find a way around it. A* (pronounced "A star") is a pathfinding algorithm, widely used in games because of its performance and accuracy. Let's take a look at an example to see how it works. Let's say we want our unit to move from point A to point B, but there's a wall in the way, and it can't go straight towards the target. So, it needs to find a way to get to point B while avoiding the wall. The following figure illustrates this scenario:

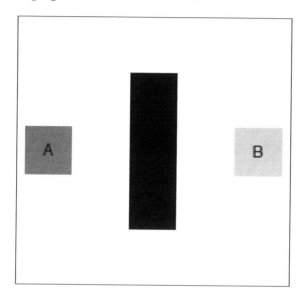

In order to find the path from point A to point B, we need to know more about the map such as the position of the obstacles. For this, we can split our whole map into small tiles, representing the whole map in a grid format. The tiles can also be of other shapes such as hexagons and triangles. Representing the whole map in a grid makes the search area more simplified, and this is an important step in pathfinding. We can now reference our map in a small 2D array.

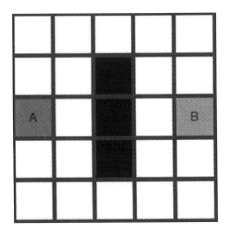

Once our map is represented by a set of tiles, we can start searching for the best path to reach the target by calculating the movement score of each tile adjacent to the starting tile, which is a tile on the map not occupied by an obstacle, and then choosing the tile with the lowest cost. We'll dive into the specifics of how we assign scores and traverse the grid in *Chapter 4, Finding Your Way*, but this is the concept of A* Pathfinding in a nutshell.

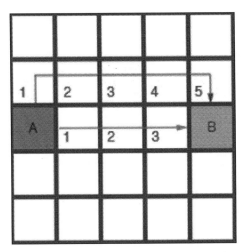

A* Pathfinding calculates the cost to move across the tiles

A* is an important pattern to know when it comes to pathfinding, but Unity also gives us a couple of features right out of the box such as automatic navigation mesh generation and the NavMesh agent, which we'll explore in the next section and then in more detail in *Chapter 4, Finding Your Way*. These features make implementing pathfinding in your games a walk in the park (no pun intended). Whether you choose to implement your own A* solution or simply go with Unity's built in NavMesh feature, will depend on your project requirements. Each have their own pros and cons, but ultimately, knowing both will allow you to make the best possible choice. With that said, let's have a quick look at NavMesh.

Using navigation mesh

Now that we've taken a brief look at A*, let's look at some possible scenarios where we might find NavMesh a fitting approach to calculate the grid. One thing that you might notice is that using a simple grid in A* requires quite a number of computations to get a path that is the shortest to the target and at the same time, avoids the obstacles. So, to make it cheaper and easier for AI characters to find a path, people came up with the idea of using waypoints as a guide to move AI characters from the start point to the target point. Let's say we want to move our AI character from point A to point B and we've set up three waypoints, as shown in the following figure:

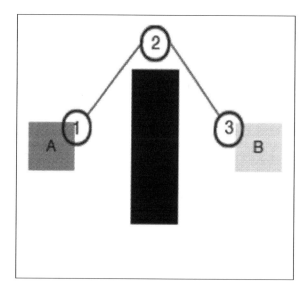

All we have to do now is to pick up the nearest waypoint and then follow its connected node leading to the target waypoint. Most of the games use waypoints for pathfinding because they are simple and quite effective in using less computation resources. However, they do have some issues. What if we want to update the obstacles in our map? We'll also have to place waypoints for the updated map again, as shown in the following figure:

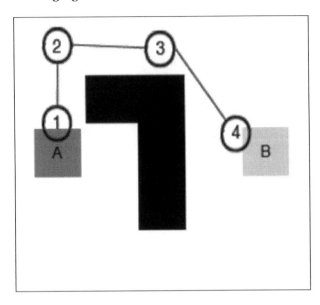

Following each node to the target can mean that the AI character moves in a series of straight lines from node to node. Look at the preceding figures; it's quite likely that the AI character will collide with the wall where the path is close to the wall. If that happens, our AI will keep trying to go through the wall to reach the next target, but it won't be able to and will get stuck there. Even though we can smooth out the path by transforming it to a spline and do some adjustments to avoid such obstacles, the problem is that the waypoints don't give any information about the environment, other than the spline is connected between the two nodes. What if our smoothed and adjusted path passes the edge of a cliff or bridge? The new path might not be a safe path anymore. So, for our AI entities to be able to effectively traverse the whole level, we're going to need a tremendous number of waypoints, which will be really hard to implement and manage.

This is a situation where a NavMesh makes the most sense. NavMesh is another graph structure that can be used to represent our world, similar to the way we did with our square tile-based grid or waypoints graph, as shown in the following screenshot:

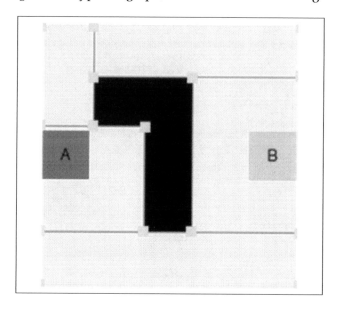

A navigation mesh uses convex polygons to represent the areas in the map that an AI entity can travel to. The most important benefit of using a navigation mesh is that it gives a lot more information about the environment than a waypoint system. Now we can adjust our path safely because we know the safe region in which our AI entities can travel. Another advantage of using a navigation mesh is that we can use the same mesh for different types of AI entities. Different AI entities can have different properties such as size, speed, and movement abilities. A set of waypoints is tailored for humans; AI may not work nicely for flying creatures or AI-controlled vehicles. These might need different sets of waypoints. Using a navigation mesh can save a lot of time in such cases.

But generating a navigation mesh programmatically based on a scene can be a somewhat complicated process. Fortunately, Unity 3.5 introduced a built-in navigation mesh generator as a Pro-only feature, but is now included for free in Unity 5 personal edition. *Chapter 4, Finding Your Way*, will look at some of the cool ways we can use Unity's NavMesh feature in your games and explore the additions and improvements that came with Unity 5.

Flocking and crowd dynamics

Many living beings such as birds, fish, insects, and land animals perform certain operations such as moving, hunting, and foraging in groups. They stay and hunt in groups, because it makes them stronger and safer from predators than pursuing goals individually. So, let's say you want a group of birds flocking, swarming around in the sky; it'll cost too much time and effort for animators to design the movement and animations of each bird. But if we apply some simple rules for each bird to follow, we can achieve emergent intelligence of the whole group with complex, global behavior.

Similarly, crowds of humans, be it on foot or vehicles, can be modeled by representing the entire crowd as an entity rather than trying to model each individual as its own agent. Each individual in the group only really needs to know where the group is heading and what their nearest neighbor is up to in order to function as part of the system.

Behavior trees

The behavior tree is another pattern used to represent and control the logic behind AI agents. They have become popular for the applications in AAA games such as Halo and Spore. Previously, we have briefly covered FSMs. They provide a very simple, yet efficient way to define the possible behaviors of an agent, based on the different states and transitions between them. However, FSMs are considered difficult to scale as they can get unwieldy fairly quickly and require a fair amount of manual setup. We need to add many states and hard-wire many transitions in order to support all the scenarios, which we want our agent to consider. So, we need a more scalable approach when dealing with large problems. This is where behavior trees come in.

Behavior trees are a collection of nodes, organized in a hierarchical order, in which nodes are connected to parents rather than states connected to each other, resembling branches on a tree, hence the name.

The basic elements of behavior trees are task nodes, where states are the main elements for FSMs. There are a few different tasks such as Sequence, Selector, and Parallel Decorator. It can be a bit daunting to track what they all do. The best way to understand this is to look at an example. Let's break the following transitions and states into tasks, as shown in the following figure:

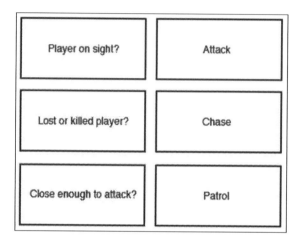

Let's look at a Selector task for this behavior tree. Selector tasks are represented with a circle and a question mark inside. The selector will evaluate each child in order, from left to right. First, it'll choose to attack the player; if the Attack task returns success, the Selector task is done and will go back to the parent node, if there is one. If the Attack task fails, it'll try the Chase task. If the Chase task fails, it'll try the Patrol task. The following figure shows the basic structure of this tree concept:

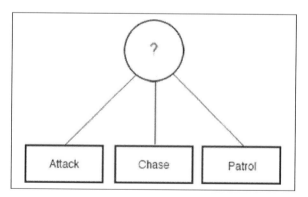

Test is one of the tasks in the behavior trees. The following diagram shows the use of Sequence tasks, denoted by a rectangle with an arrow inside it. The root selector may choose the first Sequence action. This Sequence action's first task is to check whether the player character is close enough to attack. If this task succeeds, it'll proceed with the next task, which is to attack the player. If the Attack task also returns successfully, the whole sequence will return as a success, and the selector is done with this behavior, and will not continue with other Sequence tasks. If the proximity check task fails, the Sequence action will not proceed to the Attack task, and will return a failed status to the parent selector task. Then the selector will choose the next task in the sequence, Lost or Killed Player? The following figure demonstrates this sequence:

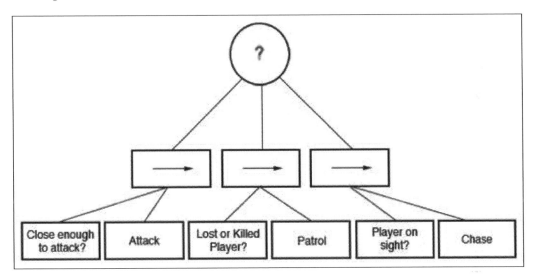

The other two common components are parallel tasks and decorators. A parallel task will execute all of its child tasks at the same time, while the Sequence and Selector tasks only execute their child tasks one by one. Decorator is another type of task that has only one child. It can change the behavior of its own child's tasks that includes whether to run its child's task or not, how many times it should run, and so on. We'll study how to implement a basic behavior tree system in Unity in *Chapter 6, Behavior Trees*.

Thinking with fuzzy logic

Finally, we arrive at fuzzy logic. Put simply, fuzzy logic refers to approximating outcomes as opposed to arriving at binary conclusions. We can use fuzzy logic and reasoning to add yet another layer of authenticity to our AI.

Let's use a generic bad guy soldier in a first person shooter as our agent to illustrate the basic concept. Whether we are using a finite state machine or a behavior tree, our agent needs to make decisions. Should I move to state x, y, or z? Will this task return true or false? Without fuzzy logic, we'd look at a binary value to determine the answer to those questions, for example, can our soldier see the player? That's a yes/no binary condition. However, if we abstract the decision making process further, we can make our soldier behave in much more interesting ways. Once we've determined that our soldier can see the player, the soldier can then "ask" itself whether it has enough ammo to kill the player, or enough health to survive being shot at, or whether there are other allies around it to assist in taking the player down. Suddenly, our AI becomes much more interesting, unpredictable, and more believable.

Summary

Game AI and academic AI have different objectives. Academic AI researches try to solve real-world problems and prove a theory without much limitation of resources. Game AI focuses on building NPCs within limited resources that seems to be intelligent to the player. The objective of AI in games is to provide a challenging opponent that makes the game more fun to play.

We learned briefly about the different AI techniques that are widely used in games such as FSMs, sensor and input systems, flocking and crowd behaviors, path following and steering behaviors, AI path finding, navigation meshes, behavior trees, and fuzzy logic.

In the following chapters, we'll look at fun and relevant ways in which you can apply these concepts to make your game more fun. We'll start off right away in *Chapter 2, Finite State Machines and You*, with our own implementation of an FSM, where we'll dive into the concepts of agents, states, and how they are applied to games.

2
Finite State Machines and You

In this chapter, we'll expand our knowledge about the FSM pattern and its uses in games and learn how to implement it in a simple Unity game. We will create a tank game with sample code, which comes with this book. We'll be dissecting the code and the components in this project. The topics we'll cover are as follows:

- Understanding Unity's state machine features
- Creating our own states and transitions
- Creating a sample scene using examples

Unity 5 introduced state machine behaviors, which are a generic expansion of the Mecanim animation states that were introduced in the 4.x cycle. These new state machine behaviors, however, are independent of the animation system, and we will learn to leverage these new features to quickly implement a state-based AI system.

In our game, the player will be able to control a tank. The enemy tanks will be moving around in the scene with reference to four waypoints. Once the player tank enters their visible range, they will start chasing us and once they are close enough to attack, they'll start shooting at our tank agent. This simple example will be a fun way to get our feet wet in the world of AI and state FSMs.

Finding uses for FSMs

Though we will primarily focus on using FSMs to implement AI in our game to make it more fun and interesting, it is important to point out that FSMs are widely used throughout game and software design and programming. In fact, the new system in Unity 5 that we'll be using was first used in the Mecanim animation system.

We can categorize many things into states in our daily lives. The most effective patterns in programming are those that mimic the simplicity of real-life designs, and FSMs are no different. Take a look around and you'll most likely notice a number of things in one of any number of possible states. For example, is there a light bulb nearby? A light bulb can be in one of two states: on or off. Let's go back to grade school for a moment and think about the time when we were learning about the different states a matter can be in. Water, for example, can be solid, liquid, or gaseous. Just like in the FSM pattern in programming, where variables can trigger a state change, water's transition from one state to another is caused by heat.

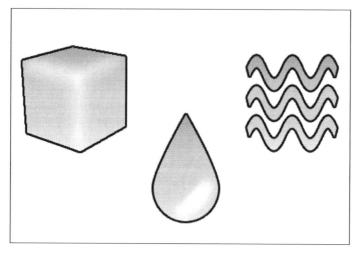

The three distinct states of water

Though there are no hard rules beyond these of our own implementation in programming design patterns, it is a characteristic of FSMs to be in one and only one state at a time. With that said, transitions allow for a "hand-off" of sorts between two states, just like ice slowly melts into water. Additionally, an agent can have multiple FSMs, driving any number of behaviors, and states can even contain state machines of their own. Think Christopher Nolan's *Inception*, but with state machines instead of dreams.

Creating state machine behaviors

Now that we're familiar with the concept of a state machine, let's get our hands dirty and start implementing our very own.

As of Unity 5.0.0f4, state machines are still part of the animation system, but worry not, they are flexible, and no animations are actually required to implement them. Don't be alarmed or confused if you see code referencing the `Animator` component or the `AnimationController` asset as it's merely a quirk of the current implementation. It's fathomable that Unity will address this in a later version, but the concepts will likely not change.

Let's fire up Unity, create a new project, and get to it.

Creating the AnimationController asset

The `AnimationController` asset is a type of asset within Unity that handles states and transitions. It is, in essence, an FSM, but it also does much more. We'll focus on the FSM portion of its functionality. An animator controller can be created from the **Assets** menu, as shown in the following image:

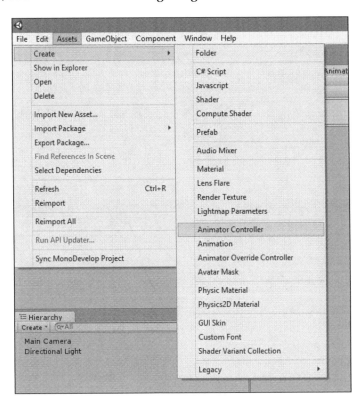

Once you create the animator controller, it will pop up in your project assets folder, ready to be named. We'll name it `TankFsm`. When you select the animator controller, unlike most other asset types, the hierarchy is blank. That is because animation controllers use their own window. You can simply click on **Open** in the hierarchy to open up the **Animator** window, or open it in the **Window** menu, as you can see in the following screenshot:

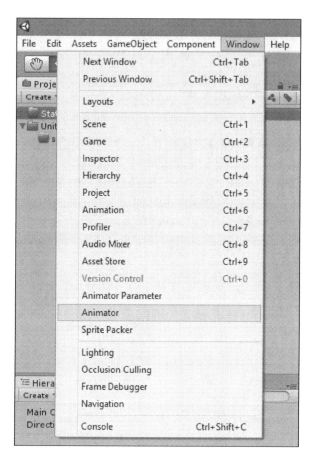

 Be sure to select **Animator** and not **Animation** as these are two different windows and features entirely.

Let's familiarize ourselves with this window before moving forward.

Layers and Parameters

Layers, as the name implies, allow us to stack different state machine levels on top of each other. This panel allows us to organize the layers easily and have a visual representation. We will not be doing much in this panel for now as it primarily relates to animation, but it's good to be familiar with it. Refer to the following screenshot of the window to find your way around the layers:

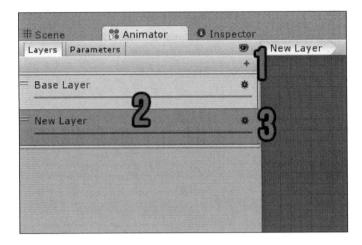

Here is a summary of the items shown in the previous screenshot:

- **Add layer**: This button creates a new layer at the bottom of the list.
- **Layer list**: These are the layers currently inside the animator controller. You can click to select a layer and drag-and-drop layers to rearrange them.
- **Layer settings**: These are animation-specific settings for the layer.

Second, we have the **Parameters** panel, which is far more relevant to our use of the animator controller. Parameters are variables that determine when to transition between states, and we can access them via scripts to drive our states. There are four types of parameters: `float`, `int`, `bool`, and `trigger`. You should already be familiar with the first three as they are primitive types in C#, but `trigger` is specific to the animator controller, not to be confused with physics triggers, which do not apply here. Triggers are just a means to trigger a transition between states explicitly.

The following screenshot shows the elements in the **Parameters** panel:

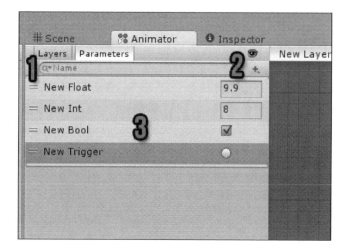

Here is a summary of the items depicted in the previous screenshot:

- **Search**: We can quickly search through our parameters here. Simply type in the name and the list will populate with the search results.

- **Add parameter**: This button lets you add new parameters. When you click on it, you must select the parameter type.

- **Parameter list**: This is the list of parameters you've created. You can assign and view their values here. You can also reorder the parameters to your liking by dragging-and-dropping them in the correct order. This is merely for organization and does not affect functionality at all.

Lastly, there is an eyeball icon, which you can click to hide the **Layers** and **Parameters** panels altogether. When the panels are closed, you can still create new layers by clicking on the **Layers** dropdown and selecting **Create New Layer**:

The animation controller inspector

The animation controller inspector is slightly different from the regular inspector found throughout Unity. While the regular inspector allows you to add components to the game objects, the animation controller inspector has a button labeled **Add Behaviour**, which allows you to add a `StateMachineBehaviour` to it. This is the main distinction between the two types of inspectors, but apart from this, it will display the serialized information for any selected state, substate, transition, or blend tree, just as the regular inspector displays the data for the selected game object and its components.

Bringing behaviors into the picture

State machine behaviors are a unique new concept in Unity 5. While states existed, conceptually, in the original implementation of Mecanim, transitions were handled behind the scenes, and you did not have much control over what happened upon entering, transitioning, or exiting a state. Unity 5 addressed this issue by introducing behaviors; they provide a built-in functionality to handle typical FSM logic.

Behaviors are sly and tricky. Though their name might lead you to believe they are related to `MonoBehaviour`, do not fall for it; if anything, these two are distant cousins at best. In fact, behaviors derive from `ScriptableObject`, not `MonoBehaviour`, so they exist only as assets, which cannot be placed in a scene or added as a component to a GameObject.

Creating our very first state

OK, so that's not entirely true since Unity creates a few default states for us in our animator controller: **New State**, **Any State**, **Entry**, and **Exit**, but let's just agree that those don't count for now, OK?

- You can select states in this window by clicking on them, and you can move them by dragging-and-dropping them anywhere in the canvas.
- Select the state named **New State** and delete it by either right-clicking and then clicking on **Delete** or simply hitting the *Delete* key on your keyboard.

- If you select the **Any State**, you'll notice that you do not have the option to delete it. The same is true for the **Entry** state. These are required states in an animator controller and have unique uses, which we'll cover up ahead.

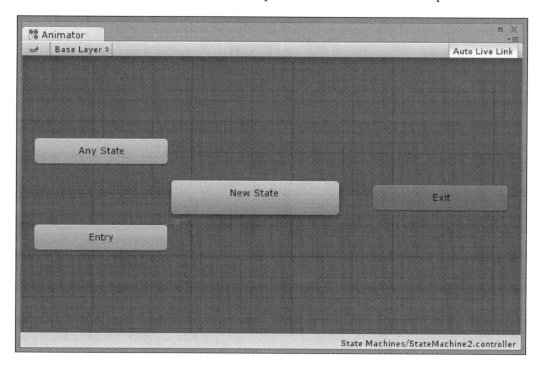

To create our (true) first state, right-click anywhere on the canvas and then select **Create State**, which opens up a few options from which we'll select **Empty**. The other two options, **From Selected Clip** and **From New Blend Tree**, are not immediately applicable to our project, so we'll skip these. Now we've officially created our first state.

Transitioning between states

You'll notice that upon creating our state, an arrow is created connecting the **Entry** state to it, and that its node is orange. Unity will automatically set default states to look orange to differentiate them from other states. When you only have one state, it is automatically selected as the default state, and as such, it is automatically connected to the entry state. You can manually select which state is the default state by right-clicking on it and then clicking on **Set as Layer Default State**. It will then become orange, and the entry state will automatically connect itself to it. The connecting arrow is a **transition connector**. Transition connectors allow us some control over how and when the transition occurs, but the connector from the entry state to the default state is unique in that it does not provide us any options since this transition happens automatically.

You can manually assign transitions between states by right-clicking on a state node and then selecting **Make Transition**. This will create a transition arrow from the state you selected to your mouse cursor. To select the destination of the transition, simply click on the destination node and that's it. Note that you cannot redirect the transitions though. We can only hope that the kind folks behind Unity add that functionality at a later point, but for now, you must remove a transition by selecting it and deleting it and then assigning an all-new transition manually.

Setting up our player tank

Open up the sample project included with this book for this chapter.

It is a good idea to group like assets together in your project folder to keep it organized. For example, you can group your state machines in a folder called StateMachines. The assets provided for this chapter are grouped for you already, so you can drop the assets and scripts you create during this chapter into the corresponding folder.

Creating the enemy tank

Let's go ahead and create an animator controller in your assets folder. This will be your enemy tank's state machine. Call it EnemyFsm.

This state machine will drive the tank's basic actions. As described earlier, in our example, the enemy can patrol, chase, and shoot the player. Let's go ahead and set up our state machine. Select the EnemyFsm asset and open up the **Animator** window.

Now, we'll go ahead and create three empty states that will conceptually and functionally represent our enemy tank's states. Name them `Patrol`, `Chase`, and `Shoot`. Once they are created and named, we'll want to make sure we have the correct default state assigned. At the moment, this will vary depending on the order in which you created and named the states, but we want the **Patrol** state to be the default state, so right-click on it and select **Set as Layer Default State**. Now it is colored orange and the **Entry** state is connected to it.

Choosing transitions

At this point, we have to make some design and logic decisions regarding the way our states will flow into each other. When we map out these transitions, we also want to keep in mind the conditions that trigger the transitions to make sure they are logical and work from a design-standpoint. Out in the wild, when you're applying these techniques on your own, different factors will play into how these transitions are handled. In order to best illustrate the topic at hand, we'll keep our transitions simple and logical:

- **Patrol**: From patrol, we can transition into chasing. We will use a chain of conditions to choose which state we'll transition into, if any.

  Can the enemy tank see the player? If yes, we go to the next step; if not, we continue with patrolling.

- **Chase**: From this state, we'll want to continue to check whether the player is within sight to continue chasing, close enough to shoot, or completely out of sight that would send us back into the patrol state.

- **Shoot**: Same as earlier, we'll want to check our range for shooting and then the line of sight to determine whether or not we can chase to get within the range.

This particular example has a simple and clean set of transition rules. If we connect our states accordingly, we'll end up with a graph looking more or less similar to this one:

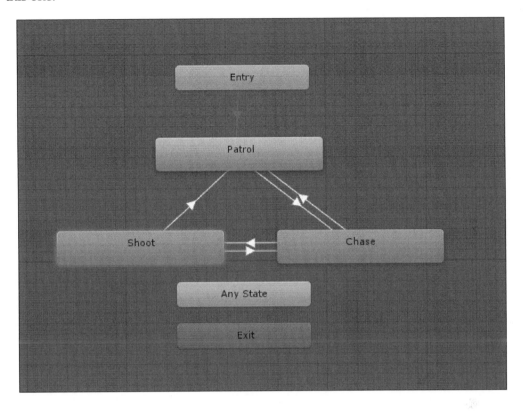

Keep in mind that the placement of the nodes is entirely up to you, and it does not affect the functionality of the state machine in any way. You try to place your nodes in a way that keeps them organized so that you can track your transitions visually.

Now that we have our states mapped out, let's assign some behaviors to them.

Making the cogs turn

This is the part I'm sure you've been waiting for. I know, I've kept you waiting, but for good reason—as we now get ready to dive into coding, we do so with a good understanding of the logical connection between the states in our FSM. Without further ado, select our **Patrol** state. In the hierarchy, you'll see a button labeled **Add Behaviour**. Clicking this gives you a context menu very similar to the **Add Component** button on regular game objects, but as we mentioned before, this button creates the oh-so-unique state machine behaviors.

Go ahead and name this behavior `TankPatrolState`. Doing so creates a script of the same name in your project and attaches it to the state we created it from. You can open this script via the project window, or by double-clicking on the name of the script in the inspector. What you'll find inside will look similar to this:

```
using UnityEngine;
using System.Collections;

public class TankPatrolState : StateMachineBehaviour {

    // OnStateEnter is called when a transition starts and the state
machine starts to evaluate this state
    //override public void OnStateEnter(Animator animator,
AnimatorStateInfo stateInfo, int layerIndex) {
    //
    //}


    // OnStateUpdate is called on each Update frame between
OnStateEnter and OnStateExit callbacks
    //override public void OnStateUpdate(Animator animator,
AnimatorStateInfo stateInfo, int layerIndex) {
    //
    //}


    // OnStateExit is called when a transition ends and the state
machine finishes evaluating this state
    //override public void OnStateExit(Animator animator,
AnimatorStateInfo stateInfo, int layerIndex) {
    //
    //}


    // OnStateMove is called right after Animator.OnAnimatorMove().
Code that processes and affects root motion should be implemented here
    //override public void OnStateMove(Animator animator,
AnimatorStateInfo stateInfo, int layerIndex) {
    //
```

```
//}

    // OnStateIK is called right after Animator.OnAnimatorIK(). Code
that sets up animation IK (inverse kinematics) should be implemented
here.
    //override public void OnStateIK(Animator animator,
AnimatorStateInfo stateInfo, int layerIndex) {
    //
    //}
}
```

Downloading the example code

You can download the example code files from your account at
`http://www.packtpub.com` for all the Packt Publishing books
you have purchased. If you purchased this book elsewhere, you
can visit `http://www.packtpub.com/support` and register to
have the files e-mailed directly to you.

Before we begin, uncomment each method. Let's break it down step by step. Unity creates this file for you, but all the methods are commented out. Essentially, the commented code acts as a guide. Much like the methods provided for you in a `MonoBehaviour`, these methods are called for you by the underlying logic. You don't need to know what's going on behind the scenes to use them; you simply have to know when they are called to leverage them. Luckily, the commented code provides a brief description of when each method is called, and the names are fairly descriptive themselves. There are two methods here we don't need to worry about: `OnStateIK` and `OnStateMove`, which are animation messages, so go ahead and delete them and save the file.

To reiterate what's stated in the code's comments, the following things happen:

- `OnStateEnter` is called when you enter the state, as soon as the transition starts
- `OnStateUpdate` is called on each frame, after MonoBehaviors update
- `OnStateExit` is called after the transition out of the state is finished

The following two states, as we mentioned, are animation-specific, so we do not use those for our purposes:

- `OnStateIK` is called just before the IK system gets updated. This is an animation and rig-specific concept.
- `OnStateMove` is used on avatars that are set up to use root motion.

Another important piece of information to note is the parameters passed into these methods:

- The animator parameter is a reference to the animator that contains this animator controller, and therefore, this state machine. By extension of that, you can fetch a reference to the game object that the animator controller is on, and from there, you can grab any other components attached to it. Remember, the state machine behavior exists only as an asset, and does not exist in the class, meaning this is the best way to get references to runtime classes, such as mono behaviors.

- The animator state info provides information about the state you're currently in, however, the uses for this are primarily focus on animation state info, so it's not as useful for our application.

- Lastly, we have the layer index, which is an integer telling us which layer within the state machine our state is in. The base layer is index 0, and each layer above that is a number higher.

Now that we understand the basics of a state machine behavior, let's get the rest of our components in order. Before we can actually see these behaviors in action, we have to go back to our state machine and add some parameters that will drive the states.

Setting conditions

We will need to provide our enemy tank with a few conditions to transitions states. These are the actual parameters that will drive the functionality.

Let's begin with the **Patrol** state. In order for our enemy tank to go from **Patrol** to **Shoot**, we need to be in range of the player, in other words, we'll be checking the distance between the enemy and the player, which is best represented by a float value. So, in your **Parameters** panel, add a float and name it `distanceFromPlayer`. We can also use this parameter to determine whether or not to go into the **Chase** state.

The **Shoot** state and the **Chase** state will share a common condition, which is whether or not the player is visible. We'll determine this via a simple raycast, which will in turn, tell us whether the player was in line-of-sight or not. The best parameter for this is a Boolean, so create a Boolean and call it `isPlayerVisible`. Leave the parameter unchecked, which means false.

Now we'll assign the conditions via the transition connectors' inspector. To do this, simply select a connector. When selected, the inspector will display some information about the current transition, and most importantly, the conditions, which show up as a list. To add a condition, simply click on the + (plus) sign:

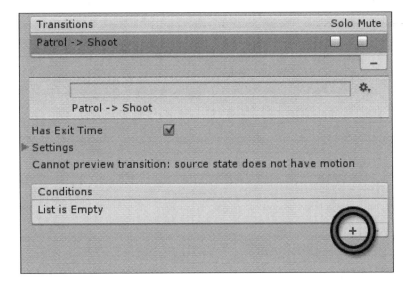

Let's tackle each transition one by one.

- Patrol to Chase
  - distanceFromPlayer < 5
  - isPlayerVisible == true

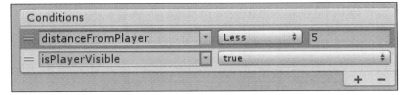

The patrol to chase transition conditions

Chase to patrol gets a bit more interesting as we have two *separate* conditions that can trigger a transition. If we were to simply add two conditions to that transition, both would have to be evaluated to true in order for the transition to occur, but we want to check whether the player is out of range or they are out of sight. Luckily, we can have multiple transitions between the same two states. Simply add another transition connection as you normally would. Right-click on the **Chase** state and then make a transition to the **Patrol** state. You'll notice that you now have two transitions listed at the top of the inspector. In addition, your transition connection indicator shows multiple arrows instead of just one to indicate that there are multiple transitions between these two states. Selecting each transition in the inspector will allow you to give each one separate condition:

- Chase to Patrol (A)
  - `distanceFromPlayer > 5`

- Chase to Patrol (B)
  - `isPlayerVisible == false`

- Chase to Shoot
  - `distanceFromPlayer < 3`
  - `isPlayerVisible == true`

- Shoot to Chase
  - `distanceFromPlayer > 3`
  - `distanceFromPlayer < 5`
  - `isPlayerVisible == true`

- Shoot to Patrol (A)
  - `distanceFromPlayer > 6`

- Shoot to Patrol (B)
  - `isPlayerVisible == false`

We now have our states and transitions set. Next, we need to create the script that will drive these values. All we need to do is set the values, and the state machine will handle the rest.

Driving parameters via code

Before going any farther, we'll need a few things from the assets we imported earlier in the chapter. For starters, go ahead and open the DemoScene folder of this chapter. You'll notice the scene is fairly stripped down and only contains an environment prefab and some waypoint transforms. Go ahead and drop in the `EnemyTankPlaceholder` prefab into the scene.

You may notice a few components that you may or may not be familiar with on the EnemyTank. We'll get a chance to thoroughly explore NavMesh and NavMeshAgent in *Chapter 4*, *Finding Your Way*, but for now, these are necessary components to make the whole thing work. What you will want to focus on is the **Animator** component which will house the state machine (animator controller) we created earlier. Go ahead and drop in the state machine into the empty slot before continuing.

We will also need a placeholder for the player. Go ahead and drop in the `PlayerTankPlaceholder` prefab as well. We won't be doing much with this for now. As with the enemy tank placeholder prefab, the player tank placeholder prefab has a few components that we can ignore for now. Simply place it in the scene and continue.

Next, you'll want to add a new component to the `EnemyTankPlaceholder` game object—the `TankAi.cs` script, which is located in the `Chapter 2` folder. If we open up the script, we'll find this inside it:

```
using UnityEngine;
using System.Collections;

public class TankAi : MonoBehaviour {
    // General state machine variables
    private GameObject player;
    private Animator animator;
    private Ray ray;
    private RaycastHit hit;
    private float maxDistanceToCheck = 6.0f;
    private float currentDistance;
    private Vector3 checkDirection;

    // Patrol state variables
    public Transform pointA;
    public Transform pointB;
    public NavMeshAgent navMeshAgent;

    private int currentTarget;
```

```
    private float distanceFromTarget;
    private Transform[] waypoints = null;

    private void Awake() {
        player = GameObject.FindWithTag("Player");
        animator = gameObject.GetComponent<Animator>();
        pointA = GameObject.Find("p1").transform;
        pointB = GameObject.Find("p2").transform;
        navMeshAgent = gameObject.GetComponent<NavMeshAgent>();
        waypoints = new Transform[2] {
            pointA,
            pointB
        };
        currentTarget = 0;
        navMeshAgent.SetDestination(waypoints[currentTarget].
position);
    }

    private void FixedUpdate() {
        //First we check distance from the player
        currentDistance = Vector3.Distance(player.transform.position,
transform.position);
        animator.SetFloat("distanceFromPlayer", currentDistance);

        //Then we check for visibility
        checkDirection = player.transform.position - transform.
position;
        ray = new Ray(transform.position, checkDirection);
        if (Physics.Raycast(ray, out hit, maxDistanceToCheck)) {
            if(hit.collider.gameObject == player){
                animator.SetBool("isPlayerVisible", true);
            } else {
                animator.SetBool("isPlayerVisible", false);
            }
        } else {
            animator.SetBool("isPlayerVisible", false);
        }

        //Lastly, we get the distance to the next waypoint target
        distanceFromTarget = Vector3.Distance(waypoints[currentTarget
].position, transform.position);
        animator.SetFloat("distanceFromWaypoint", distanceFromTarget);
    }

    public void SetNextPoint() {
```

```
        switch (currentTarget) {
            case 0:
                currentTarget = 1;
                break;
            case 1:
                currentTarget = 0;
                break;
        }
        navMeshAgent.SetDestination(waypoints[currentTarget].
position);
    }
}
```

We have a series of variables that are required to run this script, so we'll run through what they're for in order:

- `GameObject player`: This is a reference to the player placeholder prefab we dropped in earlier.

- `Animator animator`: This is the animator for our enemy tank, which contains the state machine we created.

- `Ray ray`: This is simply a declaration for a ray that we'll use in a raycast test on our `FixedUpdate` loop.

- `RaycastHit hit`: This is a declaration for the hit information we'll receive from our raycast test.

- `Float maxDistanceToCheck`: This number coincides with the value we set in our transitions inside the state machine earlier. Essentially, we are saying that we're only checking as far as this distance for the player. Beyond that, we can assume that the player is out of range.

- `Float currentDistance`: This is the current distance between the player and the enemy tanks.

You'll notice we skipped a few variables. Don't worry, we'll come back to cover these later. These are the variables we'll be using for our patrol state.

Our `Awake` method handles fetching the references to our player and animator variables. You can also declare the preceding variables as public or prefix them with the `[SerializeField]` attribute and set them via the inspector.

The `FixedUpdate` method is fairly straightforward; the first part gets the distance between the position of the player and the enemy tank. The part to pay special attention to is `animator.SetFloat("distanceFromPlayer", currentDistance)`, which passes in the information from this script into the parameter we defined earlier in our state machine. The same is true for the following section of the code, which passes in the hit result of the raycast as a Boolean. Lastly, it sets the `distanceFromTarget` variable, which we'll be using for the patrol state in the next section.

As you can see, none of the code concerns itself with how or why the state machine will handle transitions; it merely passes in the information the state machine needs, and the state machine handles the rest. Pretty cool, right?

Making our enemy tank move

You may have noticed, in addition to the variables we didn't cover yet, that our tank has no logic in place for moving. This can be easily handled with a substate machine, which is a state machine within a state. This may sound confusing at first, but we can easily break down the patrol state into substates. For our example, the Patrol state will be in one of the two substates: moving to the current waypoint and finding the next waypoint. A waypoint is essentially a destination for our agent to move toward. In order to make these changes, we'll need to go into our state machine again.

First, create a substate by clicking on an empty area on the canvas and then selecting **Create Sub-State Machine**. Since we already have our original Patrol state and all the connections that go with it, we can just drag-and-drop our **Patrol** state into our newly-created substate to merge the two. As you drag the Patrol state over the substate, you'll notice a plus sign appears by your cursor; this means you're adding one state to the other. When you drop the **Patrol** state in, the new substate will absorb it. Substates have a unique look; they are six-sided rather than rectangular. Go ahead and rename the substate to `Patrol`.

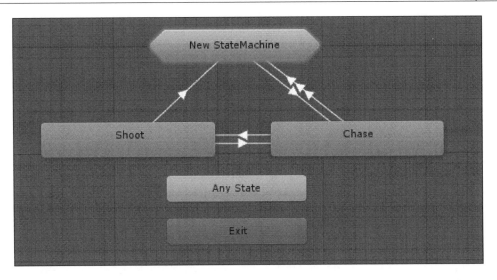

To enter a substate, simply double-click on it. Think of it as going in a level lower into the substate. The window will look fairly similar, but you will notice a few things: your **Patrol** state is connected to a node called **(Up) Base Layer**, which essentially is the connection out from this level to the upper level that the substate machine sits on, and the **Entry** state connects directly to the **Patrol** state.

Unfortunately, this is not the functionality we want as it's a closed loop that doesn't allow us to get in and out of the state into the individual waypoint states we need to create, so let's make some changes. First, we'll change the name of the substate to `PatrolEntry`. Next, we need to assign some transitions. When we enter this **Entry** state, we want to decide whether to continue moving to the current waypoint, or to find a new one. We'll represent each of the outcomes as a state, so create two states: `MovingToTarget` and `FindingNewTarget`, then create transitions from the **PatrolEntry** state to each one of the new states. Likewise, you'll want to create a transition between the two new states, meaning a transition from the MovingToTarget state to the FindingNewTarget state and vice versa. Now, add a new float parameter called `distanceFromWaypoint` and set up your conditions like this:

- PatrolEntry to MovingToTarget:
    - `distanceFromWaypoint > 1`

- PatrolEntry to FindingNewTarget:
    - `distanceFromWaypoint < 1`

- MovingToTarget to FindingNewTarget:
    - `distanceFromWaypoint < 1`

You're probably wondering why we didn't assign transition rule from the finding new target state to the MovingToTarget state. This is because we'll be executing some code via a state machine behavior and then automatically going into the MovingToTarget state without requiring any conditions. Go ahead and select the FindingNewTarget state and add a behavior and call it `SelectWaypointState`.

Open up the new script and remove all the methods, except for `OnStateEnter`. Add the following functionality to it:

```
TankAi tankAi = animator.gameObject.GetComponent<TankAi>();
tankAi.SetNextPoint();
```

What we're doing here is getting a reference to our `TankAi` script and calling its `SetNextPoint()` method. Simple enough, right?

Lastly, we need to redo our outgoing connections. Our new states don't have transitions out of this level, so we need to add one using the exact same conditions that our **PatrolEntry** state has to the **(Up) Base Layer** state. This is where **Any State** comes in handy—it allows us to transit from any state to another state, regardless of individual transition connections, so that we don't have to add transitions from each state to the **(Up) Base Layer** state; we simply add it once to the **Any State**, and we're set! Add a transition from the **Any State** to the **PatrolEntry** state and use the same conditions as the **Entry** state has to the **(Up) Base Layer** state. This is a work-around to not being able to connect directly from the **Any State** to the **(Up) Base Layer** state.

When you're done, your substate machine should look similar to this:

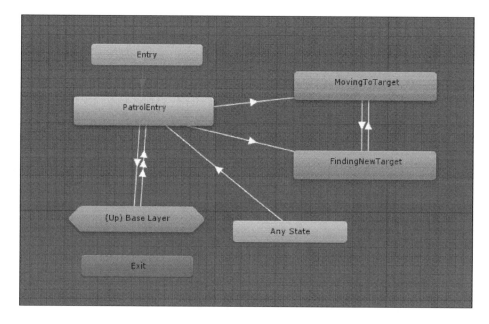

Testing

Now, all we have to do is hit play and watch our enemy tank patrol back and forth between the two provided waypoints. If we place the player in the editor in the enemy tank's path, we'll see the transition happen in the animator, out of the Patrol state, into the Chase state, and when we move the player out of range, back into the Patrol state. You'll notice our Chase and Shoot states are not fully fleshed out yet. This is because we'll be implementing these states via concepts we'll cover in *Chapter 3*, *Implementing Sensors*, and *Chapter 4*, *Finding Your Way*.

Summary

In this chapter, we learned how to implement state machines in Unity 5 using animator controller-based state machines for what will be our tank game. We learned about state machine behaviors and transitions between states. With all of these concepts covered, we then applied the simple state machine to an agent, thus creating our first artificially intelligent entity!

In the next chapter, we'll continue to build our tank game and give our agent more complex methods of sensing the world around it.

3
Implementing Sensors

In this chapter, we'll learn to implement AI behaviors using the concept of a sensory system similar to what living entities have. As we discussed earlier, a character AI system needs to have awareness of its environment such as where the obstacles are, where the enemy it's looking for is, whether the enemy is visible in the player's sight, and others. The quality of AI of our NPCs completely depends on the information it can get from the environment. Based on that information, the AI characters will decide which logic to execute. If there's not enough information for the AI, our AI characters can show strange behaviors, such as choosing the wrong places to take cover, idling, looping strange actions, and not knowing what decision to make. Search for AI glitches on YouTube, and you'll find some funny behaviors of AI characters even in AAA games.

We can detect all the environment parameters and check against our predetermined values if we want. But using a proper design pattern will help us maintain code and thus, will be easy to extend. This chapter will introduce a design pattern that we can use to implement sensory systems. We will be covering:

- What sensory systems are
- What some of the different sensory systems that exist are
- How to set up a sample tank with sensing

Basic sensory systems

The AI sensory systems emulate senses such as perspectives, sounds, and even scents to track and identify objects. In game AI sensory systems, the agents will have to examine the environment and check for such senses periodically, based on their particular interest.

The concept of a basic sensory system is that there will be two components: `Aspect` and `Sense`. Our AI characters will have senses, such as perception, smell, and touch. These senses will look out for specific aspects such as enemy and bandit. For example, you could have a patrol guard AI with a perception sense that's looking for other game objects with an enemy aspect, or it could be a zombie entity with a smell sense looking for other entities with an aspect defined as brain.

For our demo, this is basically what we are going to implement: a base interface called `Sense` that will be implemented by other custom senses. In this chapter, we'll implement perspective and touch senses. Perspective is what animals use to see the world around them. If our AI character sees an enemy, we want to be notified so that we can take some action. Likewise, with touch, when an enemy gets too close, we want to be able to sense that; almost as if our AI character can hear that the enemy is nearby. Then we'll write a minimal `Aspect` class that our senses will be looking for.

Cone of sight

In the example provided in *Chapter 2, Finite State Machines and You*, we set up our agent to detect the player tank using line of sight, which is literally a line in the form of a raycast. A raycast is a feature in Unity that allows you to determine which objects are intersected by a line cast from a point toward a given direction. While this is a fairly efficient to handle visual detection in a simple way, it doesn't accurately model the way vision works for most entities. An alternative to using line of sight is using a cone-shaped field of vision. As the following figure illustrates, the field of vision is literally modeled using a cone shape. This can be in 2D or 3D, as appropriate for your type of game.

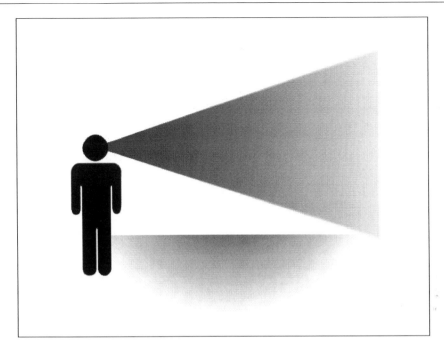

The preceding figure illustrates the concept of a cone of sight. In this case, beginning with the source, that is, the agent's eyes, the cone grows, but becomes less accurate with the distance, as represented by the fading color of the cone.

The actual implementation of the cone can vary from a basic overlap test to a more complex realistic model, mimicking eyesight. In the simple implementation, it is only necessary to test whether an object overlaps with the cone of sight, ignoring distance or periphery. The complex implementation mimics eyesight more closely; as the cone widens away from the source, the field of vision grows, but the chance of getting to see things toward the edges of the cone diminishes compared to those near the center of the source.

Hearing, feeling, and smelling using spheres

One very simple, yet effective way of modeling sounds, touch, and smell is via the use of spheres. For sounds, for example, we imagine the center as being the source, and the loudness dissipating the farther from the center the listener is. Inversely, the listener can be modeled instead of, or in addition to, the source of the sound. The listener's hearing is represented with a sphere, and the sounds closest to the listener are more likely to be "heard". We can modify the size and position of the sphere relative to our agent to accommodate feeling and smelling.

The following figure visualizes our sphere and how our agent fits into the setup:

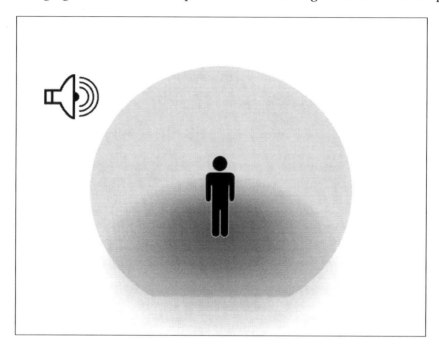

As with sight, the probability of an agent registering the sensory event can be modified, based on the distance from the sensor or as a simple overlap event, where the sensory event is always detected as long as the source overlaps the sphere.

Expanding AI through omniscience

Truth be told, omniscience is really a way to make your AI cheat. While your agent doesn't necessarily know everything, it simply means that they can know anything. In some ways, this can seem like the antithesis to realism, but often the simple solution is the best solution. Allowing our agent access to seemingly hidden information about their surroundings or other entities in the game world can be a powerful tool to give it an extra layer of complexity.

In games, we tend to model abstract concepts using concrete values. For example, we may represent a player's health with a numeric value ranging from 0 to 100. Giving our agent access to this type of information allows it to make realistic decisions, even though having access to that information is not realistic. You can also think of omniscience as your agent being able to "use the force" or sense events in your game world without having to "physically" experience them.

Getting creative with sensing

While these are among the most basic ways an agent can see, hear, and perceive their environment, they are by no means the only ways to implement these senses. If your game calls for other types of sensing, feel free to combine these patterns together. Want to use a cylinder or a sphere to represent a field of vision? Go for it. Want to use boxes to represent the sense of smell? Sniff away!

Setting up the scene

Now we have to get a little bit of setup out of the way to start implementing the topics we've discussed. We need to get our scene ready with environment objects, our agents, and some other items to help us see what the code is doing:

1. Let's create a few walls to block the line of sight from our AI character to the enemy. These will be short but wide cubes grouped under an empty game object called `Obstacles`.

2. Add a plane to be used as a floor.

3. Then, we add a directional light so that we can see what is going on in our scene.

We will be going over this next part in detail throughout the chapter, but basically, we will use a simple tank model for our player, and a simple cube for our AI character. We will also have a `Target` object to show us where the tank will move to in our scene. Our scene hierarchy will look similar to the following screenshot:

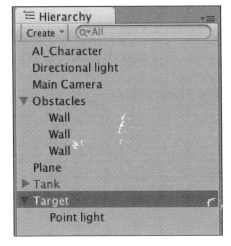

The hierarchy

Now we will position the tank, AI character, and walls randomly in our scene. Increase the size of the plane to something that looks good. Fortunately, in this demo, our objects float, so nothing will fall off the plane. Also, be sure to adjust the camera so that we can have a clear view of the following scene:

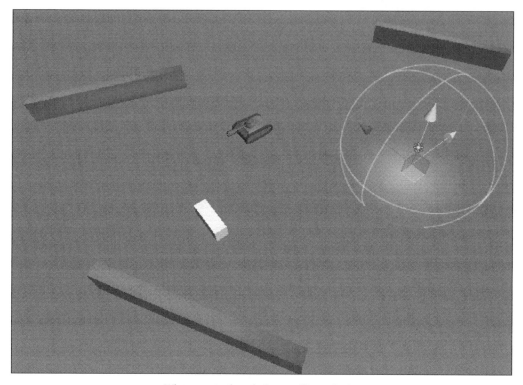

Where our tank and player will wander in

Now that we have the basics set up, we'll look at how to implement the tank, AI character, and aspects for our player character.

Setting up the player tank and aspect

Our `Target` object is a simple sphere object with the mesh render disabled. We have also created a point light and made it a child of our `Target` object. Make sure the light is centered, or it will not be very helpful for us.

Look at the following code in the `Target.cs` file:

```
using UnityEngine;
using System.Collections;

public class Target : MonoBehaviour {

  public Transform targetMarker;

  void Update () {
    int button = 0;
    //Get the point of the hit position when the mouse is being
// clicked.
    if (Input.GetMouseButtonDown(button)) {
      Ray ray = Camera.main.ScreenPointToRay(Input.mousePosition);
      RaycastHit hitInfo;
      if (Physics.Raycast(ray.origin, ray.direction, out hitInfo)) {
        Vector3 targetPosition = hitInfo.point;
        targetMarker.position = targetPosition;
      }
    }
  }
}
```

Attach this script to our `Target` object, which is what we assign in the inspector to the `targetMarker` variable. The script detects the mouse click event and then, using the raycasting technique, detects the mouse click point on the plane in the 3D space. After that it updates the `Target` object to that position in our scene.

Implementing the player tank

Our player tank is the simple tank model we used in *Chapter 2, Finite State Machines and You*, with a non-kinematic rigid body component attached. The rigid body component is needed in order to generate trigger events whenever we do collision detection with any AI characters. The first thing we need to do is to assign the tag Player to our tank.

The tank is controlled by the PlayerTank script, which we will create in a moment. This script retrieves the target position on the map and updates its destination point and the direction accordingly.

The code in the PlayerTank.cs file is shown as follows:

```
using UnityEngine;
using System.Collections;

public class PlayerTank : MonoBehaviour {
  public Transform targetTransform;
  private float movementSpeed, rotSpeed;

  void Start () {
    movementSpeed = 10.0f;
    rotSpeed = 2.0f;
  }

  void Update () {
    //Stop once you reached near the target position
    if (Vector3.Distance(transform.position,
      targetTransform.position) < 5.0f)
      return;

    //Calculate direction vector from current position to target
//position
    Vector3 tarPos = targetTransform.position;
    tarPos.y = transform.position.y;
    Vector3 dirRot = tarPos - transform.position;

    //Build a Quaternion for this new rotation vector
    //using LookRotation method
    Quaternion tarRot = Quaternion.LookRotation(dirRot);

    //Move and rotate with interpolation
```

```
transform.rotation= Quaternion.Slerp(transform.rotation,
    tarRot, rotSpeed * Time.deltaTime);

transform.Translate(new Vector3(0, 0,
    movementSpeed * Time.deltaTime));
  }
}
```

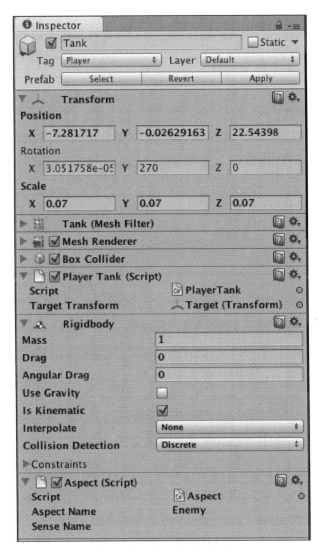

Properties of our tank object

The preceding screenshot gives us a snapshot of our script in the inspector once applied to our tank.

This script retrieves the position of the `Target` object on the map and updates its destination point and the direction accordingly. After we assign this script to our tank, be sure to assign our `Target` object to the `targetTransform` variable.

Implementing the Aspect class

Next, let's take a look at the `Aspect.cs` class. Aspect is a very simple class with just one public property called `aspectName`. That's all of the variables we need in this chapter. Whenever our AI character senses something, we'll check against this with `aspectName` to see whether it's the aspect that the AI has been looking for.

The code in the `Aspect.cs` file is shown as follows:

```
using UnityEngine;
using System.Collections;

public class Aspect : MonoBehaviour {
  public enum aspect {
    Player,
    Enemy
  }
  public aspect aspectName;
}
```

Attach this aspect script to our player tank and set the `aspectName` property as `Enemy`, as shown in the following image:

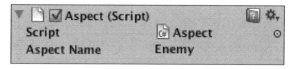

Setting which aspect to look out for

Creating an AI character

Our AI character will be roaming around the scene in a random direction. It'll have two senses:

- The perspective sense will check whether the enemy aspect is within a set visible range and distance

- Touch sense will detect if the enemy aspect has collided with the box collider, soon to be surrounding our AI character

As we have seen previously, our player tank will have the Enemy aspect. So, these senses will be triggered when they detect the player tank.

The code in the Wander.cs file can be shown as follows:

```
using UnityEngine;
using System.Collections;

public class Wander : MonoBehaviour {
  private Vector3 tarPos;

  private float movementSpeed = 5.0f;
  private float rotSpeed = 2.0f;
  private float minX, maxX, minZ, maxZ;

  // Use this for initialization
  void Start () {
    minX = -45.0f;
    maxX = 45.0f;

    minZ = -45.0f;
    maxZ = 45.0f;

    //Get Wander Position
    GetNextPosition();
  }

  // Update is called once per frame
  void Update () {
    // Check if we're near the destination position
    if (Vector3.Distance(tarPos, transform.position) <= 5.0f)
      GetNextPosition(); //generate new random position

    // Set up quaternion for rotation toward destination
    Quaternion tarRot = Quaternion.LookRotation(tarPos -
        transform.position);

    // Update rotation and translation
    transform.rotation = Quaternion.Slerp(transform.rotation, tarRot,
        rotSpeed * Time.deltaTime);

    transform.Translate(new Vector3(0, 0,
```

```
            movementSpeed * Time.deltaTime));
    }

    void GetNextPosition() {
      tarPos = new Vector3(Random.Range(minX, maxX), 0.5f,
          Random.Range(minZ, maxZ));
    }
}
```

The Wander script generates a new random position in a specified range whenever the AI character reaches its current destination point. The Update method will then rotate our enemy and move it toward this new destination. Attach this script to our AI character so that it can move around in the scene.

Using the Sense class

The Sense class is the interface of our sensory system that the other custom senses can implement. It defines two virtual methods, Initialize and UpdateSense, which will be implemented in custom senses, and are executed from the Start and Update methods, respectively.

The code in the Sense.cs file can be shown as follows:

```
using UnityEngine;
using System.Collections;

public class Sense : MonoBehaviour {
  public bool bDebug = true;
  public Aspect.aspect aspectName = Aspect.aspect.Enemy;
  public float detectionRate = 1.0f;

  protected float elapsedTime = 0.0f;

  protected virtual void Initialize() { }
  protected virtual void UpdateSense() { }

  // Use this for initialization
  void Start () {
    elapsedTime = 0.0f;
    Initialize();
  }

  // Update is called once per frame
```

```
    void Update () {
      UpdateSense();
    }
  }
```

The basic properties include its detection rate to execute the sensing operation as well as the name of the aspect it should look for. This script will not be attached to any of our objects.

Giving a little perspective

The perspective sense will detect whether a specific aspect is within its field of view and visible distance. If it sees anything, it will take the specified action.

The code in the Perspective.cs file can be shown as follows:

```
using UnityEngine;
using System.Collections;

public class Perspective : Sense {
  public int FieldOfView = 45;
  public int ViewDistance = 100;

  private Transform playerTrans;
  private Vector3 rayDirection;

  protected override void Initialize() {

    //Find player position
    playerTrans =

  GameObject.FindGameObjectWithTag("Player").transform;
  }

  // Update is called once per frame
  protected override void UpdateSense() {
    elapsedTime += Time.deltaTime;

    // Detect perspective sense if within the detection rate
    if (elapsedTime >= detectionRate) DetectAspect();
  }

  //Detect perspective field of view for the AI Character
  void DetectAspect() {
```

```
        RaycastHit hit;

        //Direction from current position to player position
        rayDirection = playerTrans.position -
            transform.position;

        //Check the angle between the AI character's forward
        //vector and the direction vector between player and AI
        if ((Vector3.Angle(rayDirection, transform.forward)) <
    FieldOfView) {
            // Detect if player is within the field of view
            if (Physics.Raycast(transform.position, rayDirection,
                out hit, ViewDistance)) {
              Aspect aspect =
              hit.collider.GetComponent<Aspect>();

              if (aspect != null) {
                //Check the aspect
                if (aspect.aspectName == aspectName) {
                  print("Enemy Detected");
                }
              }
            }
        }
    }
```

We need to implement the Initialize and UpdateSense methods that will be called from the Start and Update methods of the parent Sense class, respectively. Then, in the DetectAspect method, we first check the angle between the player and the AI's current direction. If it's in the field of view range, we shoot a ray in the direction where the player tank is located. The ray length is the value of visible distance property. The Raycast method will return when it first hits another object. Then, we'll check against the aspect component and the aspect name. This way, even if the player is in the visible range, the AI character will not be able to see if it's hidden behind the wall.

The OnDrawGizmos method draws lines based on the perspective field of view angle and viewing distance so that we can see the AI character's line of sight in the editor window during play testing. Attach this script to our AI character and be sure that the aspect name is set to Enemy.

This method can be illustrated as follows:

```
void OnDrawGizmos() {
    if (playerTrans == null) return;

    Debug.DrawLine(transform.position, playerTrans.position, Color.
red);

    Vector3 frontRayPoint = transform.position +
        (transform.forward * ViewDistance);

    //Approximate perspective visualization
    Vector3 leftRayPoint = frontRayPoint;
    leftRayPoint.x += FieldOfView * 0.5f;

    Vector3 rightRayPoint = frontRayPoint;
    rightRayPoint.x -= FieldOfView * 0.5f;

    Debug.DrawLine(transform.position, frontRayPoint, Color.green);

    Debug.DrawLine(transform.position, leftRayPoint, Color.green);

    Debug.DrawLine(transform.position, rightRayPoint, Color.green);
    }
}
```

Touching is believing

Another sense we're going to implement is `Touch.cs`, which is triggered when the player entity is within a certain area near the AI entity. Our AI character has a box collider component and its `IsTrigger` flag is on.

We need to implement the `OnTriggerEnter` event that will be fired whenever the collider component is collided with another collider component. Since our tank entity also has a collider and rigid body components, collision events will be raised as soon as the colliders of the AI character and player tank are collided.

The code in the `Touch.cs` file can be shown as follows:

```
using UnityEngine;
using System.Collections;

public class Touch : Sense {
    void OnTriggerEnter(Collider other) {
        Aspect aspect = other.GetComponent<Aspect>();
```

```
        if (aspect != null) {
          //Check the aspect
          if (aspect.aspectName == aspectName) {
            print("Enemy Touch Detected");
          }
        }
      }
    }
  }
```

We implement the `OnTriggerEnter` event to be fired whenever the collider component is collided with another collider component. Since our tank entity also has a collider and the rigid body components, collision events will be raised as soon as the colliders of the AI character and the player tank are collided. Our trigger can be seen in the following screenshot:

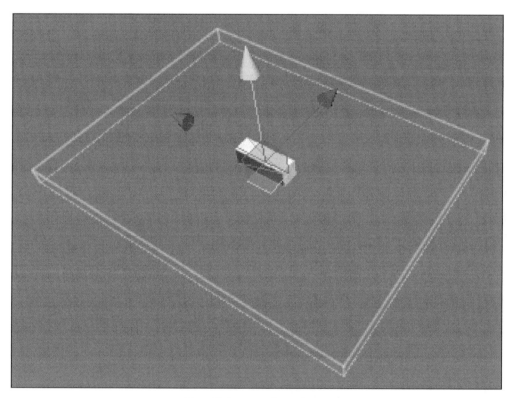

The collider around our player

The preceding screenshot shows the box collider of our enemy AI that we'll use to implement the touch sense. In the following screenshot, we see how our AI character is set up:

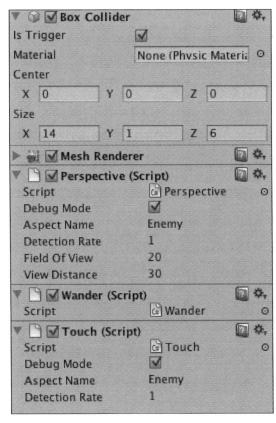

The properties of our player

Inside the `OnTriggerEnter` method, we access the aspect component of the other collided entity and check whether the name of the aspect is the aspect this AI character is looking for. And, for demo purposes, we just print out that the enemy aspect has been detected by touch sense. We can also implement other behaviors in real projects; maybe the player will turn over to an enemy and start chasing, attacking, and so on.

Testing the results

Play the game in Unity3D and move the player tank near the wandering AI character by clicking on the ground. You should see the **Enemy touch detected** message in the console log window whenever our AI character gets close to our player tank.

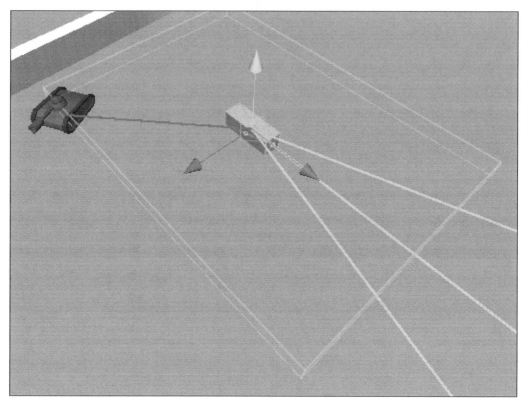

Our player and tank in action

The preceding screenshot shows an AI agent with touch and perspective senses looking for an enemy aspect. Move the player tank in front of the AI character, and you'll get the **Enemy detected** message. If you go to the editor view while running the game, you should see the debug drawings rendered. This is because of the OnDrawGizmos method implemented in the perspective Sense class.

Summary

This chapter introduced the concept of using sensors in implementing game AI and implemented two senses, perspective and touch, for our AI character. The sensory system is just part of the decision-making system of the whole AI system. We can use the sensory system in combination with a behavior system to execute certain behaviors for certain senses. For example, we can use an FSM to change to Chase and Attack states from the Patrol state once we have detected that there's an enemy within the line of sight. We'll also cover how to apply behavior tree systems in *Chapter 6, Behavior Trees*.

In the next chapter, we'll look at how to implement flocking behaviors in Unity3D as well as the Craig Reynold's flocking algorithm.

4
Finding Your Way

Obstacle avoidance is a simple behavior for the AI entities to reach a target point. It's important to note that the specific behavior implemented in this chapter is meant to be used for behaviors such as crowd simulation, where the main objective of each agent entity is just to avoid the other agents and reach the target. There's no consideration on what would be the most efficient and shortest path. We'll learn about the A* Pathfinding algorithm in the next section.

In this chapter, we will cover the following topics:

- Path following and steering
- A custom A* Pathfinding implementation
- Unity's built-in NavMesh

Following a path

Paths are usually created by connecting waypoints together. So, we'll set up a simple path, as shown in the following screenshot, and then make our cube entity follow along the path smoothly. Now, there are many ways to build such a path. The one we are going to implement here could arguably be the simplest one. We'll write a script called Path.cs and store all the waypoint positions in a Vector3 array. Then, from the editor, we'll enter those positions manually. It's bit of a tedious process right now. One option is to use the position of an empty game object as waypoints. Or, if you want, you can create your own editor plugins to automate these kind of tasks, but that is outside the scope of this book. For now, it should be fine to just enter the waypoint information manually, since the number of waypoints that we are creating here are not that substantial.

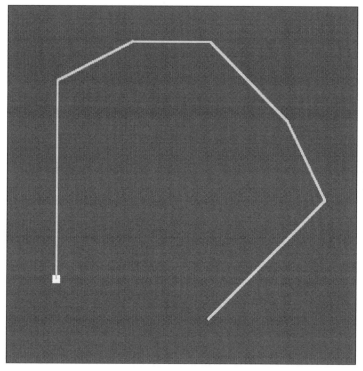

An object path

First, we create an empty game entity and add our path script component, as shown in the following screenshot:

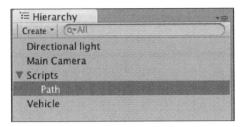

The organized Hierarchy

Then, we populate our **Point A** variable with all the points we want to be included in our path:

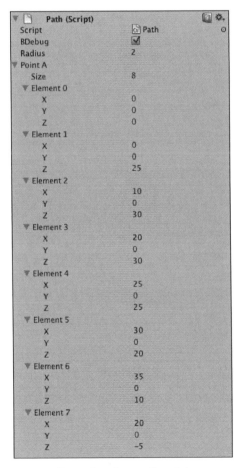

Properties of our path script

The preceding list shows the waypoints needed to create the path that was described earlier. The other two properties are debug mode and radius. If the debug mode property is checked, the path formed by the positions entered will be drawn as gizmos in the editor window. The radius property is a range value for the path-following entities to use so that they can know when they've reached a particular waypoint if they are in this radius range. Since to reach an exact position can be pretty difficult, this range radius value provides an effective way for the path-following agents to navigate through the path.

The path script

So, let's take a look at the path script itself. It will be responsible for managing the path for our objects. Look at the following code in the Path.cs file:

```
using UnityEngine;
using System.Collections;

public class Path : MonoBehaviour {
  public bool bDebug = true;
  public float Radius = 2.0f;
  public Vector3[] pointA;

  public float Length {
    get {
      return pointA.Length;
    }
  }

  public Vector3 GetPoint(int index) {
    return pointA[index];
  }

  void OnDrawGizmos() {
    if (!bDebug) return;

    for (int i = 0; i <pointA.Length; i++) {
      if (i + 1<pointA.Length) {
        Debug.DrawLine(pointA[i], pointA[i + 1],
          Color.red);
      }
    }
  }
}
```

As you can see, this is a very simple script. It has a `Length` property that returns the length and size of the waypoint array if requested. The `GetPoint` method returns the `Vector3` position of a particular waypoint at a specified index in the array. Then, we have the `OnDrawGizmos` method that is called by Unity frame to draw components in the editor environment. The drawing here won't be rendered in the game view unless gizmos, located in the top-right corner of the game view, are turned on.

Using the path follower

Next, we have our vehicle entity, which is just a simple cube object in this example. We can replace the cube later with whatever 3D models we want. After we create the script, we add the `VehicleFollowing` script component, as shown in the following screenshot:

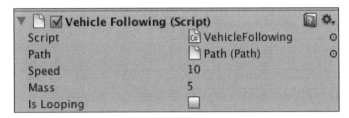

The properties of our VehicleFollowing script

The script takes a couple of parameters. First is the reference to the path object it needs to follow. Then, the `Speed` and `Mass` properties, which are needed to calculate its acceleration properly. The `IsLooping` flag is a flag that makes this entity follow the path continuously if it's checked. Let's take a look at the following code in the `VehicleFollowing.cs` file:

```
using UnityEngine;
using System.Collections;

public class VehicleFollowing : MonoBehaviour {
    public Path path;
    public float speed = 20.0f;
    public float mass = 5.0f;
    public bool isLooping = true;

    //Actual speed of the vehicle
    private float curSpeed;

    private int curPathIndex;
    private float pathLength;
    private Vector3 targetPoint;

    Vector3 velocity;
```

First, we initialize the properties and set up the direction of our `velocity` vector with the entity's `forward` vector in the `Start` method, as shown in the following code:

```
void Start () {
    pathLength = path.Length;
    curPathIndex = 0;

    //get the current velocity of the vehicle
    velocity = transform.forward;
}
```

There are only two methods that are important in this script, the `Update` and `Steer` methods. Let's take a look at the following code:

```
void Update () {
    //Unify the speed
    curSpeed = speed * Time.deltaTime;

    targetPoint = path.GetPoint(curPathIndex);

    //If reach the radius within the path then move to next
      //point in the path
        if (Vector3.Distance(transform.position, targetPoint) <
          path.Radius) {
          //Don't move the vehicle if path is finished
        if (curPathIndex < pathLength - 1) curPathIndex++;
          else if (isLooping) curPathIndex = 0;
          else return;
    }

    //Move the vehicle until the end point is reached in
      //the path
        if (curPathIndex >= pathLength ) return;

    //Calculate the next Velocity towards the path
        if (curPathIndex >= pathLength-1&& !isLooping)
          velocity += Steer(targetPoint, true);
          else velocity += Steer(targetPoint);

    //Move the vehicle according to the velocity
      transform.position += velocity;
    //Rotate the vehicle towards the desired Velocity
      transform.rotation = Quaternion.LookRotation(velocity);
}
```

In the `Update` method, we check whether our entity has reached a particular waypoint by calculating the distance between its current position and the path's radius range. If it's in the range, we just increase the index to look it up from the waypoints array. If it's the last waypoint, we check if the `isLooping` flag is set. If it is set, we set the target to the starting waypoint; otherwise, we just stop at that point. Though, if we wanted, we could make it so that our object turned around and went back the way it came. In the next part, we will calculate the acceleration from the `Steer` method. Then, we rotate our entity and update the position according to the speed and direction of the velocity:

```
//Steering algorithm to steer the vector towards the target
public Vector3 Steer(Vector3 target,
   bool bFinalPoint = false) {
//Calculate the directional vector from the current
   //position towards the target point
Vector3 desiredVelocity = (target -transform.position);
float dist = desiredVelocity.magnitude;

//Normalise the desired Velocity
desiredVelocity.Normalize();

//Calculate the velocity according to the speed
if (bFinalPoint&&dist<10.0f) desiredVelocity *=
   (curSpeed * (dist / 10.0f));
   else desiredVelocity *= curSpeed;

//Calculate the force Vector
Vector3 steeringForce = desiredVelocity - velocity;
Vector3 acceleration = steeringForce / mass;

return acceleration;
 }
}
```

The steer method takes the parameter target, which is a Vector3 position representing the final waypoint in the path. The first thing we do is to calculate the remaining distance from the current position to the target position. The target position vector minus the current position vector gives a vector toward the target position vector. The magnitude of this vector is the remaining distance. We then normalize this vector just to preserve the direction property. Now, if this is the final waypoint, and the distance is less than 10 of a number we just decided to use, we slow down the velocity gradually according to the remaining distance to our point until the velocity finally becomes zero, otherwise, we just update the target velocity with the specified speed value. By subtracting the current velocity vector from this target velocity vector, we can calculate the new steering vector. Then, by dividing this vector with the mass value of our entity, we get the acceleration.

If you run the scene, you should see your cube object following the path. You can also see the path that is drawn in the editor view. Play around with the speed and mass value of the follower and radius values of the path and see how they affect the overall behavior of the system.

Avoiding obstacles

In this section, we'll set up a scene, as shown in the following screenshot, and make our AI entity avoid the obstacles while trying to reach the target point. The algorithm presented here using the raycasting method is very simple, so it can only avoid the obstacles blocking the path in front of it. The following screenshot will show us our scene:

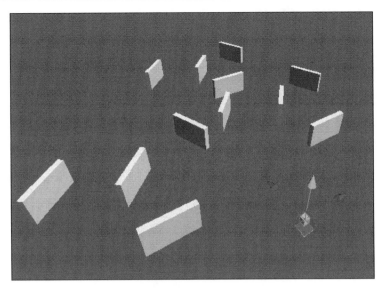

A sample scene setup

To create this, we make a few cube entities and group them under an empty game object called Obstacles. We also create another cube object called Agent and give it our obstacle avoidance script. We then create a ground plane object to assist in finding a target position.

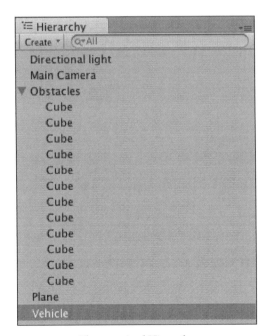

The organized Hierarchy

It is worth noting that this `Agent` object is not a pathfinder. As such, if we set too many walls up, our `Agent` might have a hard time finding the target. Try a few wall setups and see how our `Agent` performs.

Adding a custom layer

We will now add a custom layer to our object. To add a new layer, we navigate to **Edit | Project Settings | Tags**. Assign the name `Obstacles` to **User Layer 8**. Now, we go back to our cube entity and set its `layer` property to `Obstacles`.

Creating a new layer

This is our new layer, which is added to Unity. Later, when we do the raycasting to detect obstacles, we'll only check for these entities using this particular layer. This way, we can ignore some objects that are not obstacles that are being hit by a ray, such as bushes or vegetation.

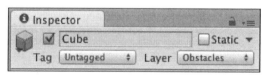

Assigning our new layer

For larger projects, our game objects probably already have a layer assigned to them. So, instead of changing the object's layer to `Obstacles`, we would instead make a list using bitmaps of layers for our cube entity to use when detecting obstacles. We will talk more about bitmaps in the next section.

Layers are most commonly used by cameras to render a part of the scene, and by lights to illuminate only some parts of the scene. But, they can also be used by raycasting to selectively ignore colliders or create collisions. You can learn more about this at `http://docs.unity3d.com/Documentation/Components/Layers.html`.

Implementing the avoidance logic

Now it is time to make the script that will help our cube entity avoid these walls.

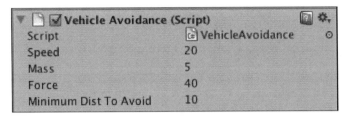

The properties of our VehicleAvoidance (script)

As usual, we first initialize our entity script with the default properties and draw a GUI text in our `OnGUI` method. Let's take a look at the following code in the `VehicleAvoidance.cs` file:

```
using UnityEngine;
using System.Collections;

public class VehicleAvoidance : MonoBehaviour {
  public float speed = 20.0f;
  public float mass = 5.0f;
  public float force = 50.0f;
  public float minimumDistToAvoid = 20.0f;

  //Actual speed of the vehicle
  private float curSpeed;
  private Vector3 targetPoint;

  // Use this for initialization
  void Start () {
    mass = 5.0f;
    targetPoint = Vector3.zero;
  }

  void OnGUI() {
    GUILayout.Label("Click anywhere to move the vehicle.");
  }
```

Then in our `Update` method, we update the agent entity's position and rotation, based on the direction vector returned by the `AvoidObstacles` method:

```
//Update is called once per frame
void Update () {
  //Vehicle move by mouse click
  RaycastHit hit;
  var ray = Camera.main.ScreenPointToRay
      (Input.mousePosition);

  if (Input.GetMouseButtonDown(0) &&
    Physics.Raycast(ray, out hit, 100.0f)) {
    targetPoint = hit.point;
  }

  //Directional vector to the target position
  Vector3 dir = (targetPoint - transform.position);
  dir.Normalize();

  //Apply obstacle avoidance
  AvoidObstacles(ref dir);

  //...

}
```

The first thing we do in our `Update` method is retrieve the mouse click position so that we can move our AI entity. We do this by shooting a ray from the camera in the direction it's looking. Then, we take the point where the ray hit the ground plane as our target position. Once we get the target position vector, we can calculate the direction vector by subtracting the current position vector from the target position vector. Then, we call the `AvoidObstacles` method and pass in this direction vector:

```
//Calculate the new directional vector to avoid
  //the obstacle
public void AvoidObstacles(ref Vector3 dir) {
  RaycastHit hit;

  //Only detect layer 8 (Obstacles)
  int layerMask = 1<<8;

  //Check that the vehicle hit with the obstacles within
    //it's minimum distance to avoid
  if (Physics.Raycast(transform.position,
    transform.forward, out hit,
```

```
            minimumDistToAvoid, layerMask)) {
      //Get the normal of the hit point to calculate the
        //new direction
        Vector3 hitNormal = hit.normal;
        hitNormal.y = 0.0f; //Don't want to move in Y-Space

        //Get the new directional vector by adding force to
        //vehicle's current forward vector
       dir = transform.forward + hitNormal * force;
      }
   }
 }
```

The AvoidObstacles method is also quite simple. The only trick to note here is that raycasting interacts selectively with the Obstacles layer that we specified at **User Layer 8** in our Unity TagManager. The Raycast method accepts a layer mask parameter to determine which layers to ignore and which to consider during raycasting. Now, if you look at how many layers you can specify in TagManager, you'll find a total of 32 layers. Therefore, Unity uses a 32-bit integer number to represent this layer mask parameter. For example, the following would represent a zero in 32 bits:

```
0000 0000 0000 0000 0000 0000 0000 0000
```

By default, Unity uses the first eight layers as built-in layers. So, when you raycast without using a layer mask parameter, it'll raycast against all those eight layers, which could be represented like the following in a bitmask:

```
0000 0000 0000 0000 0000 0000 1111 1111
```

Our Obstacles layer was set at layer 8 (9th index), and we only want to raycast against this layer. So, we'd like to set up our bitmask in the following way:

```
0000 0000 0000 0000 0000 0001 0000 0000
```

The easiest way to set up this bitmask is by using the bit shift operators. We only need to place the 'on' bit or 1 at the 9th index, which means we can just move that bit 8 places to the left. So, we use the left shift operator to move the bit 8 places to the left, as shown in the following code:

```
int layerMask = 1<<8;
```

If we wanted to use multiple layer masks, say layer 8 and layer 9, an easy way would be to use the bitwise OR operator like this:

```
int layerMask = (1<<8) | (19);
```

You can also find a good discussion on using layermasks on Unity3D online. The question and answer site can be found at `http://answers.unity3d.com/questions/8715/how-do-i-use-layermasks.html`.

Once we have the layer mask, we call the `Physics.Raycast` method from the current entity's position and in the forward direction. For the length of the ray, we use our `minimumDistToAvoid` variable so that we'll only avoid those obstacles that are being hit by the ray within this distance.

Then, we take the normal vector of the hit ray, multiply it with the force vector, and add it to the current direction of our entity to get the new resultant direction vector, which we return from this method.

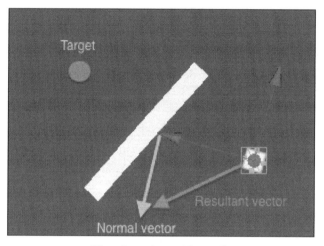

The cube entity avoids a wall

Then in our `Update` method, we use this new direction after avoiding obstacles to rotate the AI entity and update the position according to the speed value:

```
void Update () {

    //...

    //Don't move the vehicle when the target point
      //is reached
    if (Vector3.Distance(targetPoint,
      transform.position) < 3.0f) return;

      //Assign the speed with delta time
```

```
curSpeed = speed * Time.deltaTime;

//Rotate the vehicle to its target
  //directional vector
var rot = Quaternion.LookRotation(dir);
transform.rotation = Quaternion.Slerp
  (transform.rotation, rot, 5.0f *
  Time.deltaTime);

//Move the vehicle towards
  transform.position += transform.forward *
    curSpeed;
}
```

A* Pathfinding

Next up, we'll be implementing the A* algorithm in a Unity environment using C#. The A* Pathfinding algorithm is widely used in games and interactive applications even though there are other algorithms, such as Dijkstra's algorithm, because of its simplicity and effectiveness. We've briefly covered this algorithm previously in *Chapter 1*, *The Basics of AI in Games*, but let's review the algorithm again from an implementation perspective.

Revisiting the A* algorithm

Let's review the A* algorithm again before we proceed to implement it in the next section. First, we'll need to represent the map in a traversable data structure. While many structures are possible, for this example, we will use a 2D grid array. We'll implement the GridManager class later to handle this map information. Our GridManager class will keep a list of the Node objects that are basically titles in a 2D grid. So, we need to implement that Node class to handle things such as node type (whether it's a traversable node or an obstacle), cost to pass through and cost to reach the goal Node, and so on.

We'll have two variables to store the nodes that have been processed and the nodes that we have to process. We'll call them closed list and open list, respectively. We'll implement that list type in the `PriorityQueue` class. And then finally, the following A* algorithm will be implemented in the `AStar` class. Let's take a look at it:

1. We begin at the starting node and put it in the open list.

2. As long as the open list has some nodes in it, we'll perform the following processes:

    1. Pick the first node from the open list and keep it as the current node. (This is assuming that we've sorted the open list and the first node has the least cost value, which will be mentioned at the end of the code.)

    2. Get the neighboring nodes of this current node that are not obstacle types, such as a wall or canyon that can't be passed through.

    3. For each neighbor node, check if this neighbor node is already in the closed list. If not, we'll calculate the total cost (F) for this neighbor node using the following formula:

       ```
       F = G + H
       ```

    4. In the preceding formula, G is the total cost from the previous node to this node and H is the total cost from this node to the final target node.

    5. Store this cost data in the neighbor node object. Also, store the current node as the parent node as well. Later, we'll use this parent node data to trace back the actual path.

    6. Put this neighbor node in the open list. Sort the open list in ascending order, ordered by the total cost to reach the target node.

    7. If there's no more neighbor nodes to process, put the current node in the closed list and remove it from the open list.

    8. Go back to step 2.

Once you have completed this process your current node should be in the target goal node position, but only if there's an obstacle free path to reach the goal node from the start node. If it is not at the goal node, there's no available path to the target node from the current node position. If there's a valid path, all we have to do now is to trace back from current node's parent node until we reach the start node again. This will give us a path list of all the nodes that we chose during our pathfinding process, ordered from the target node to the start node. We then just reverse this path list since we want to know the path from the start node to the target goal node.

This is a general overview of the algorithm we're going to implement in Unity using C#. So let's get started.

Implementation

We'll implement the preliminary classes that were mentioned before, such as the Node, GridManager, and PriorityQueue classes. Then, we'll use them in our main AStar class.

Implementing the Node class

The Node class will handle each tile object in our 2D grid, representing the maps shown in the Node.cs file:

```
using UnityEngine;
using System.Collections;
using System;

public class Node : IComparable {
  public float nodeTotalCost;
  public float estimatedCost;
  public bool bObstacle;
  public Node parent;
  public Vector3 position;

  public Node() {
    this.estimatedCost = 0.0f;
    this.nodeTotalCost = 1.0f;
    this.bObstacle = false;
    this.parent = null;
  }

  public Node(Vector3 pos) {
    this.estimatedCost = 0.0f;
    this.nodeTotalCost = 1.0f;
    this.bObstacle = false;
    this.parent = null;
    this.position = pos;
  }

  public void MarkAsObstacle() {
    this.bObstacle = true;
  }
```

The Node class has properties, such as the cost values (G and H), flags to mark whether it is an obstacle, its positions, and parent node. The nodeTotalCost is G, which is the movement cost value from starting node to this node so far and the estimatedCost is H, which is total estimated cost from this node to the target goal node. We also have two simple constructor methods and a wrapper method to set whether this node is an obstacle. Then, we implement the CompareTo method as shown in the following code:

```
public int CompareTo(object obj) {
    Node node = (Node)obj;
    //Negative value means object comes before this in the sort
      //order.
    if (this.estimatedCost < node.estimatedCost)
      return -1;
    //Positive value means object comes after this in the sort
      //order.
    if (this.estimatedCost > node.estimatedCost) return 1;
    return 0;
  }
}
```

This method is important. Our Node class inherits from IComparable because we want to override this CompareTo method. If you can recall what we discussed in the previous algorithm section, you'll notice that we need to sort our list of node arrays based on the total estimated cost. The ArrayList type has a method called Sort. This method basically looks for this CompareTo method, implemented inside the object (in this case, our Node objects) from the list. So, we implement this method to sort the node objects based on our estimatedCost value.

 The IComparable.CompareTo method, which is a .NET framework feature, can be found at http://msdn.microsoft.com/en-us/library/system.icomparable.compareto.aspx.

Establishing the priority queue

The PriorityQueue class is a short and simple class to make the handling of the nodes' ArrayList easier, as shown in the following PriorityQueue.cs class:

```
using UnityEngine;
using System.Collections;

public class PriorityQueue {
```

```
    private ArrayList nodes = new ArrayList();

    public int Length {
      get { return this.nodes.Count; }
    }

    public bool Contains(object node) {
      return this.nodes.Contains(node);
    }

    public Node First() {
      if (this.nodes.Count > 0) {
        return (Node)this.nodes[0];
      }
      return null;
    }

    public void Push(Node node) {
      this.nodes.Add(node);
      this.nodes.Sort();
    }

    public void Remove(Node node) {
      this.nodes.Remove(node);
      //Ensure the list is sorted
      this.nodes.Sort();
    }
  }
```

The preceding code listing should be easy to understand. One thing to notice is that after adding or removing node from the nodes' ArrayList, we call the Sort method. This will call the Node object's CompareTo method and will sort the nodes accordingly by the estimatedCost value.

Setting up our grid manager

The GridManager class handles all the properties of the grid, representing the map. We'll keep a singleton instance of the GridManager class as we need only one object to represent the map, as shown in the following GridManager.cs file:

```
    using UnityEngine;
    using System.Collections;

    public class GridManager : MonoBehaviour {
```

```
      private static GridManager s_Instance = null;

      public static GridManager instance {
        get {
          if (s_Instance == null) {
            s_Instance = FindObjectOfType(typeof(GridManager))
                as GridManager;
            if (s_Instance == null)
              Debug.Log("Could not locate a GridManager " +
                  "object. \n You have to have exactly " +
                  "one GridManager in the scene.");
          }
          return s_Instance;
        }
      }
```

We look for the `GridManager` object in our scene and if found, we keep it in our `s_Instance` static variable:

```
      public int numOfRows;
      public int numOfColumns;
      public float gridCellSize;
      public bool showGrid = true;
      public bool showObstacleBlocks = true;

      private Vector3 origin = new Vector3();
      private GameObject[] obstacleList;
      public Node[,] nodes { get; set; }
      public Vector3 Origin {
        get { return origin; }
      }
```

Next, we declare all the variables; we'll need to represent our map, such as number of rows and columns, the size of each grid tile, and some Boolean variables to visualize the grid and obstacles as well as to store all the nodes present in the grid, as shown in the following code:

```
      void Awake() {
        obstacleList = GameObject.FindGameObjectsWithTag("Obstacle");
        CalculateObstacles();
      }
      // Find all the obstacles on the map
      void CalculateObstacles() {
        nodes = new Node[numOfColumns, numOfRows];
        int index = 0;
```

```
    for (int i = 0; i < numOfColumns; i++) {
      for (int j = 0; j < numOfRows; j++) {
        Vector3 cellPos = GetGridCellCenter(index);
        Node node = new Node(cellPos);
        nodes[i, j] = node;
        index++;
      }
    }
    if (obstacleList != null && obstacleList.Length > 0) {
      //For each obstacle found on the map, record it in our list
      foreach (GameObject data in obstacleList) {
        int indexCell = GetGridIndex(data.transform.position);
        int col = GetColumn(indexCell);
        int row = GetRow(indexCell);
        nodes[row, col].MarkAsObstacle();
      }
    }
  }
```

We look for all the game objects with an Obstacle tag and put them in
our obstacleList property. Then we set up our nodes' 2D array in the
CalculateObstacles method. First, we just create the normal node objects with
default properties. Just after that, we examine our obstacleList. Convert their
position into row-column data and update the nodes at that index to be obstacles.

The GridManager class has a couple of helper methods to traverse the grid and get
the grid cell data. The following are some of them with a brief description of what
they do. The implementation is simple, so we won't go into the details.

The GetGridCellCenter method returns the position of the grid cell in world
coordinates from the cell index, as shown in the following code:

```
public Vector3 GetGridCellCenter(int index) {
  Vector3 cellPosition = GetGridCellPosition(index);
  cellPosition.x += (gridCellSize / 2.0f);
  cellPosition.z += (gridCellSize / 2.0f);
  return cellPosition;
}

public Vector3 GetGridCellPosition(int index) {
  int row = GetRow(index);
  int col = GetColumn(index);
```

```
        float xPosInGrid = col * gridCellSize;
        float zPosInGrid = row * gridCellSize;
        return Origin + new Vector3(xPosInGrid, 0.0f, zPosInGrid);
    }
```

The GetGridIndex method returns the grid cell index in the grid from the given position:

```
    public int GetGridIndex(Vector3 pos) {
        if (!IsInBounds(pos)) {
            return -1;
        }
        pos -= Origin;
        int col = (int)(pos.x / gridCellSize);
        int row = (int)(pos.z / gridCellSize);
        return (row * numOfColumns + col);
    }

    public bool IsInBounds(Vector3 pos) {
        float width = numOfColumns * gridCellSize;
        float height = numOfRows* gridCellSize;
        return (pos.x >= Origin.x &&  pos.x <= Origin.x + width &&
            pos.x <= Origin.z + height && pos.z >= Origin.z);
    }
```

The GetRow and GetColumn methods return the row and column data of the grid cell from the given index:

```
    public int GetRow(int index) {
        int row = index / numOfColumns;
        return row;
    }

    public int GetColumn(int index) {
        int col = index % numOfColumns;
        return col;
    }
```

Another important method is GetNeighbours, which is used by the AStar class to retrieve the neighboring nodes of a particular node:

```
    public void GetNeighbours(Node node, ArrayList neighbors) {
        Vector3 neighborPos = node.position;
        int neighborIndex = GetGridIndex(neighborPos);

        int row = GetRow(neighborIndex);
```

```
        int column = GetColumn(neighborIndex);

        //Bottom
        int leftNodeRow = row - 1;
        int leftNodeColumn = column;
        AssignNeighbour(leftNodeRow, leftNodeColumn, neighbors);

        //Top
        leftNodeRow = row + 1;
        leftNodeColumn = column;
        AssignNeighbour(leftNodeRow, leftNodeColumn, neighbors);

        //Right
        leftNodeRow = row;
        leftNodeColumn = column + 1;
        AssignNeighbour(leftNodeRow, leftNodeColumn, neighbors);

        //Left
        leftNodeRow = row;
        leftNodeColumn = column - 1;
        AssignNeighbour(leftNodeRow, leftNodeColumn, neighbors);
    }

    void AssignNeighbour(int row, int column, ArrayList neighbors) {
        if (row != -1 && column != -1 &&
            row < numOfRows && column < numOfColumns) {
          Node nodeToAdd = nodes[row, column];
          if (!nodeToAdd.bObstacle) {
            neighbors.Add(nodeToAdd);
          }
        }
    }
```

First, we retrieve the neighboring nodes of the current node in the left, right, top, and bottom, all four directions. Then, inside the `AssignNeighbour` method, we check the node to see whether it's an obstacle. If it's not, we push that neighbor node to the referenced array list, `neighbors`. The next method is a debug aid method to visualize the grid and obstacle blocks:

```
    void OnDrawGizmos() {
        if (showGrid) {
          DebugDrawGrid(transform.position, numOfRows, numOfColumns,
              gridCellSize, Color.blue);
        }
```

```
        Gizmos.DrawSphere(transform.position, 0.5f);
        if (showObstacleBlocks) {
          Vector3 cellSize = new Vector3(gridCellSize, 1.0f,
            gridCellSize);
          if (obstacleList != null && obstacleList.Length > 0) {
            foreach (GameObject data in obstacleList) {
              Gizmos.DrawCube(GetGridCellCenter(
                  GetGridIndex(data.transform.position)), cellSize);
            }
          }
        }
      }

      public void DebugDrawGrid(Vector3 origin, int numRows, int
        numCols,float cellSize, Color color) {
        float width = (numCols * cellSize);
        float height = (numRows * cellSize);

        // Draw the horizontal grid lines
        for (int i = 0; i < numRows + 1; i++) {
          Vector3 startPos = origin + i * cellSize * new Vector3(0.0f,
            0.0f, 1.0f);
          Vector3 endPos = startPos + width * new Vector3(1.0f, 0.0f,
            0.0f);
          Debug.DrawLine(startPos, endPos, color);
        }

        // Draw the vertical grid lines
        for (int i = 0; i < numCols + 1; i++) {
          Vector3 startPos = origin + i * cellSize * new Vector3(1.0f,
            0.0f, 0.0f);
          Vector3 endPos = startPos + height * new Vector3(0.0f, 0.0f,
            1.0f);
          Debug.DrawLine(startPos, endPos, color);
        }
      }
    }
```

Gizmos can be used to draw visual debugging and setup aids inside the editor
scene view. The OnDrawGizmos method is called every frame by the engine. So, if
the debug flags, showGrid and showObstacleBlocks, are checked, we just draw
the grid with lines and obstacle cube objects with cubes. Let's not go through the
DebugDrawGrid method, which is quite simple.

You can learn more about gizmos in the Unity reference documentation at `http://docs.unity3d.com/Documentation/ScriptReference/Gizmos.html`.

Diving into our A* implementation

The `AStar` class is the main class that will utilize the classes we have implemented so far. You can go back to the algorithm section if you want to review this. We start with our `openList` and `closedList` declarations, which are of the `PriorityQueue` type, as shown in the `AStar.cs` file:

```
using UnityEngine;
using System.Collections;

public class AStar {
    public static PriorityQueue closedList, openList;
```

Next, we implement a method called `HeuristicEstimateCost` to calculate the cost between the two nodes. The calculation is simple. We just find the direction vector between the two by subtracting one position vector from another. The magnitude of this resultant vector gives the direct distance from the current node to the goal node:

```
private static float HeuristicEstimateCost(Node curNode,
    Node goalNode) {
  Vector3 vecCost = curNode.position - goalNode.position;
  return vecCost.magnitude;
}
```

Next, we have our main `FindPath` method:

```
public static ArrayList FindPath(Node start, Node goal) {
  openList = new PriorityQueue();
  openList.Push(start);
  start.nodeTotalCost = 0.0f;
  start.estimatedCost = HeuristicEstimateCost(start, goal);

  closedList = new PriorityQueue();
  Node node = null;
```

We initialize our open and closed lists. Starting with the start node, we put it in our open list. Then we start processing our open list:

```
while (openList.Length != 0) {
  node = openList.First();
  //Check if the current node is the goal node
```

```
        if (node.position == goal.position) {
          return CalculatePath(node);
        }

        //Create an ArrayList to store the neighboring nodes
        ArrayList neighbours = new ArrayList();

        GridManager.instance.GetNeighbours(node, neighbours);

        for (int i = 0; i < neighbours.Count; i++) {
          Node neighbourNode = (Node)neighbours[i];

          if (!closedList.Contains(neighbourNode)) {
            float cost = HeuristicEstimateCost(node,
                neighbourNode);

            float totalCost = node.nodeTotalCost + cost;
            float neighbourNodeEstCost = HeuristicEstimateCost(
                neighbourNode, goal);

            neighbourNode.nodeTotalCost = totalCost;
            neighbourNode.parent = node;
            neighbourNode.estimatedCost = totalCost +
                neighbourNodeEstCost;

            if (!openList.Contains(neighbourNode)) {
              openList.Push(neighbourNode);
            }
          }
        }
      //Push the current node to the closed list
      closedList.Push(node);
      //and remove it from openList
      openList.Remove(node);
    }

    if (node.position != goal.position) {
      Debug.LogError("Goal Not Found");
      return null;
    }
    return CalculatePath(node);
}
```

This code implementation resembles the algorithm that we have previously discussed, so you can refer back to it if you are not clear of certain things. Perform the following steps:

1. Get the first node of our `openList`. Remember our `openList` of nodes is always sorted every time a new node is added. So, the first node is always the node with the least estimated cost to the goal node.

2. Check whether the current node is already at the goal node. If so, exit the `while` loop and build the `path` array.

3. Create an array list to store the neighboring nodes of the current node being processed. Use the `GetNeighbours` method to retrieve the neighbors from the grid.

4. For every node in the `neighbors` array, we check whether it's already in `closedList`. If not, we calculate the cost values, update the node properties with the new cost values as well as the parent node data, and put it in `openList`.

5. Push the current node to `closedList` and remove it from `openList`. Go back to step 1.

If there are no more nodes in `openList`, our current node should be at the target node if there's a valid path available. Then, we just call the `CalculatePath` method with the current node parameter:

```
private static ArrayList CalculatePath(Node node) {
  ArrayList list = new ArrayList();
  while (node != null) {
    list.Add(node);
    node = node.parent;
  }
  list.Reverse();
  return list;
  }
}
```

The `CalculatePath` method traces through each node's parent node object and builds an array list. It gives an array list with nodes from the target node to the start node. Since we want a path array from the start node to the target node, we just call the `Reverse` method.

So, this is our `AStar` class. We'll write a test script in the following code to test all this and then set up a scene to use them in.

Implementing a Test Code class

This class will use the `AStar` class to find the path from the start node to the goal node, as shown in the following `TestCode.cs` file:

```
using UnityEngine;
using System.Collections;

public class TestCode : MonoBehaviour {
   private Transform startPos, endPos;
   public Node startNode { get; set; }
   public Node goalNode { get; set; }

   public ArrayList pathArray;

   GameObject objStartCube, objEndCube;
   private float elapsedTime = 0.0f;
   //Interval time between pathfinding
   public float intervalTime = 1.0f;
```

First, we set up the variables that we'll need to reference. The `pathArray` is to store the nodes array returned from the `AStar` `FindPath` method:

```
void Start () {
   objStartCube = GameObject.FindGameObjectWithTag("Start");
   objEndCube = GameObject.FindGameObjectWithTag("End");

   pathArray = new ArrayList();
   FindPath();
}

void Update () {
   elapsedTime += Time.deltaTime;
   if (elapsedTime >= intervalTime) {
     elapsedTime = 0.0f;
     FindPath();
   }
}
```

In the `Start` method, we look for objects with the `Start` and `End` tags and initialize our `pathArray`. We'll be trying to find our new path at every interval that we set to our `intervalTime` property in case the positions of the start and end nodes have changed. Then, we call the `FindPath` method:

```
void FindPath() {
  startPos = objStartCube.transform;
  endPos = objEndCube.transform;

  startNode = new Node(GridManager.instance.GetGridCellCenter(
      GridManager.instance.GetGridIndex(startPos.position)));

  goalNode = new Node(GridManager.instance.GetGridCellCenter(
      GridManager.instance.GetGridIndex(endPos.position)));

  pathArray = AStar.FindPath(startNode, goalNode);
}
```

Since we implemented our pathfinding algorithm in the `AStar` class, finding a path has now become a lot simpler. First, we take the positions of our start and end game objects. Then, we create new `Node` objects using the helper methods of `GridManager` and `GetGridIndex` to calculate their respective row and column index positions inside the grid. Once we get this, we just call the `AStar.FindPath` method with the start node and goal node and store the returned array list in the local `pathArray` property. Next, we implement the `OnDrawGizmos` method to draw and visualize the path found:

```
void OnDrawGizmos() {
  if (pathArray == null)
    return;

  if (pathArray.Count > 0) {
    int index = 1;
    foreach (Node node in pathArray) {
      if (index < pathArray.Count) {
        Node nextNode = (Node)pathArray[index];
        Debug.DrawLine(node.position, nextNode.position,
          Color.green);
        index++;
      }
    }
  }
}
```

We look through our `pathArray` and use the `Debug.DrawLine` method to draw the lines connecting the nodes from the `pathArray`. With this, we'll be able to see a green line connecting the nodes from start to end, forming a path, when we run and test our program.

Setting up our sample scene

We are going to set up a scene that looks something similar to the following screenshot:

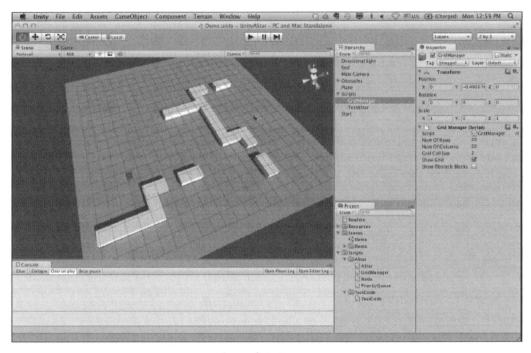

A sample test scene

We'll have a directional light, the start and end game objects, a few obstacle objects, a plane entity to be used as ground, and two empty game objects in which we put our `GridManager` and `TestAStar` scripts. This is our scene hierarchy:

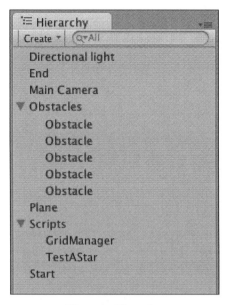

The scene Hierarchy

Create a bunch of cube entities and tag them as `Obstacle`. We'll be looking for objects with this tag when running our pathfinding algorithm.

The Obstacle node

Create a cube entity and tag it as Start.

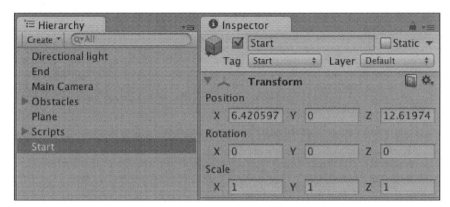

The Start node

Then, create another cube entity and tag it as End.

The End node

Now, create an empty game object and attach the `GridManager` script. Set the name as `GridManager` because we use this name to look for the `GridManager` object from our script. Here, we can set up the number of rows and columns for our grid as well as the size of each tile.

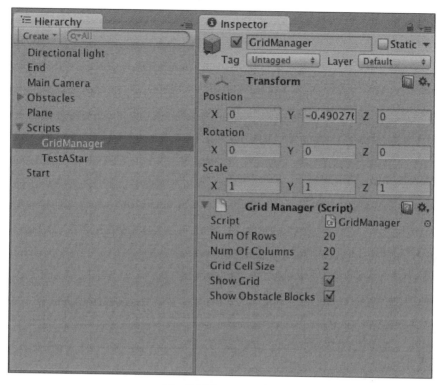

The GridManager script

Testing all the components

Let's hit the play button and see our A* Pathfinding algorithm in action. By default, once you play the scene, Unity will switch to the **Game** view. Since our pathfinding visualization code is written for the debug drawn in the editor view, you'll need to switch back to the **Scene** view or enable **Gizmos** to see the path found.

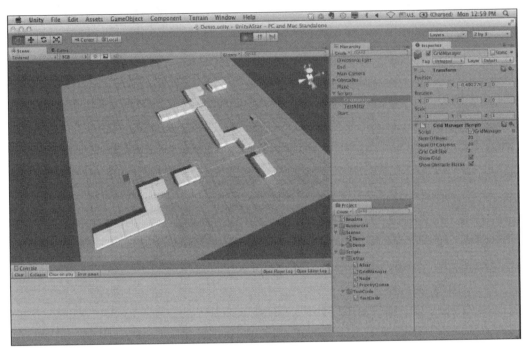

Found path one

Now, try to move the start or end node around in the scene using the editor's movement gizmo (not in the **Game** view, but the **Scene** view).

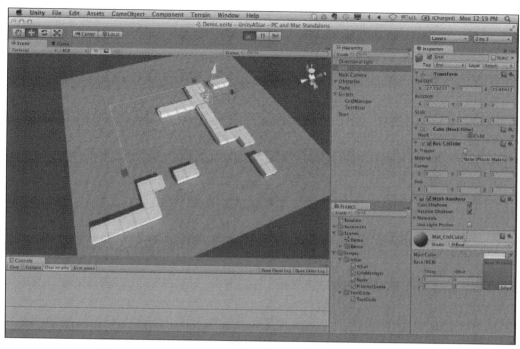

Found path two

You should see the path updated accordingly if there's a valid path from the start node to the target goal node, dynamically in real time. You'll get an error message in the console window if there's no path available.

Navigation mesh

Next, we'll learn how to use Unity's built-in navigation mesh generator that can make pathfinding for AI agents a lot easier. As of Unity 5, NavMesh is available to all the users. Previously a Unity Pro-only feature, NavMesh is now a part of the Personal Edition of Unity. We were briefly exposed to Unity's NavMesh in *Chapter 2, Finite State Machines and You*, which relied on a NavMesh agent for movement in testing our state machine. Now, we will finally dive in and explore all that this system has to offer. AI pathfinding needs representation of the scene in a particular format. We've seen that using a 2D grid (array) for A* Pathfinding on a 2D map. AI agents need to know where the obstacles are, especially the static obstacles. Dealing with collision avoidance between dynamically moving objects is another subject, primarily known as steering behaviors. Unity has a built-in navigation feature to generate a NavMesh that represents the scene in a context that makes sense for our AI agents to find the optimum path to the target. This chapter comes with a Unity project that has four scenes in it. You should open it in Unity and see how it works to get a feeling of what we are going to build. Using this sample project, we'll study how to create a NavMesh and use it with AI agents inside our own scenes.

Setting up the map

To get started, we'll build a simple scene, as shown in the following screenshot:

A scene with obstacles

This is the first scene in our sample project called `NavMesh01-Simple.scene`. You can use a plane as a ground object and several cube entities as the wall objects. Later, we'll put in some AI agents (we'll be turning to our trusted tank for this example as well) to go to the mouse-clicked position, as in an **RTS (real-time strategy)** game.

Navigation Static

Once we've added the walls and ground, it's important to mark them as **Navigation Static** so that the NavMesh generator knows that these are the static obstacle objects to avoid. Only game objects marked as navigation static will be taken into account when building the NavMesh, so be sure to mark any environment elements accordingly. To do this, select all those objects, click on the **Static** dropdown, and choose **Navigation Static**, as shown in the following screenshot:

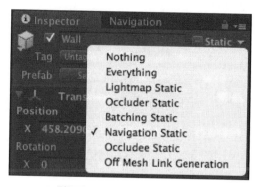

The Navigation Static property

Baking the navigation mesh

Now we're done with our scene. Let's bake the NavMesh. Firstly, we need to open the navigation window. Navigate to **Window | Navigation**. The navigation window is broken up into three different sections. The first, **Object**, looks similar to the following screenshot:

The navigation object window

The **Object** tab of the navigation window is simply a shortcut to selecting objects and modifying their navigation-related attributes. Toggling between the **Scene Filter** options, **All**, **Mesh Renderers**, and **Terrains**, will filter out objects in your hierarchy accordingly so that you can easily select objects and change their **Navigation Static** and **Generate OffMeshLinks** flags as well as set their **Navigation Area**.

The second tab is the **Bake** tab. It looks similar to the following screenshot:

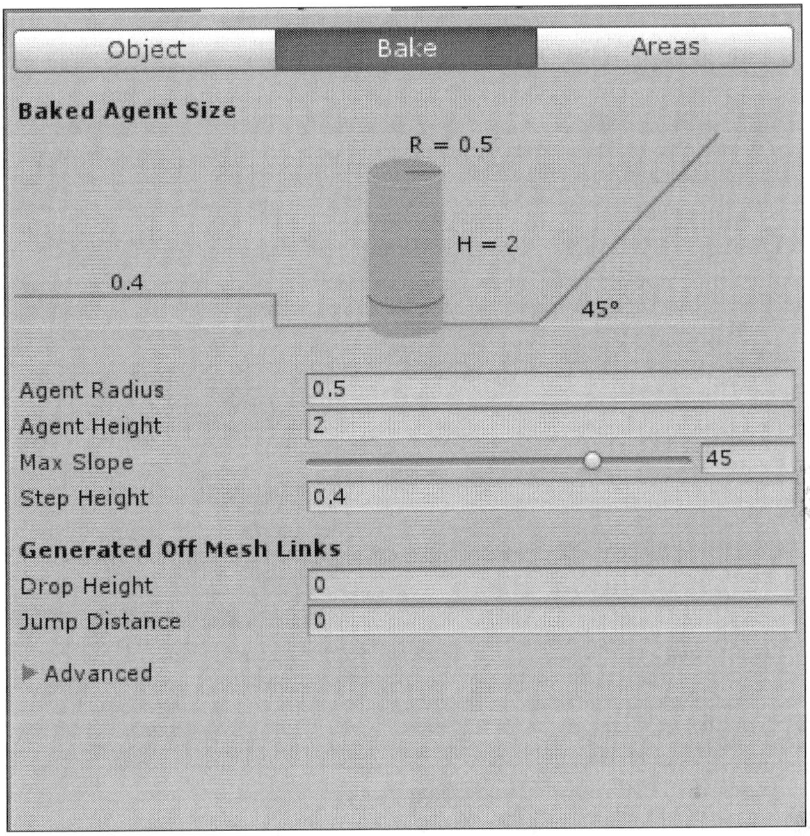

If you've ever stumbled across this tab prior to Unity 5, you may notice that it now looks a bit different. Unity 5 added a visualizer to see exactly what each setting does. Let's take a look at what each of these settings does:

- **Agent Radius**: The Unity documentation describes it best as the NavMesh agent's "personal space". The agent will use this radius when it needs to avoid other objects.

- **Agent Height**: This is similar to radius, except for the fact that it designates the height of the agent that determines if it can pass under obstacles, and so on.

- **Max Slope**: This is the max angle that the agent can walk up to. The agent will not be able to walk up the slopes that are steeper than this value.

- **Step Height**: Agents can step or climb over obstacles of this value or less.

The second category of values only applies when you checked **Generate OffMeshLinks** when building your NavMesh. This simply means that the agent will be able to potentially navigate the NavMesh even when gaps are present due to physical distance:

- **Drop Height**: Fairly straightforward, this is the distance an agent can jump down. For example, the height of a cliff from which an agent will be "brave enough" to jump down.

- **Jump Distance**: This is the distance an agent will jump between offmesh links.

The third and final set of parameters is not the one that you would generally need to change:

- **Manual Voxel Size**: Unity's NavMesh implementation relies on voxels. This setting lets you increase the accuracy of the NavMesh generation. A lower number is more accurate, while a larger number is less accurate, but faster.

- **Min Region Area**: Areas smaller than this will simply be culled away, and ignored.

- **Height Mesh**: It gives you a higher level of detail in vertical placement of your agent at the cost of speed at runtime.

The third and last tab is the **Areas** tab, which looks similar to the following screenshot:

If you recall, the **Object** tab allows you to assign the specific objects to certain areas, for example, grass, sand, water, and so on. You can then assign an area mask to an agent, which allows you to pick areas agents can or cannot walk through. The cost parameter affects the likeliness of an agent to attempt to traverse that area. Agents will prefer lower-cost paths when possible.

We will keep our example simple, but feel free to experiment with the various settings. For now, we'll leave the default values and just click on **Bake** at the bottom of the window. You should see a progress bar baking the NavMesh for your scene, and after a while, you'll see your NavMesh in your scene, as shown in following diagram:

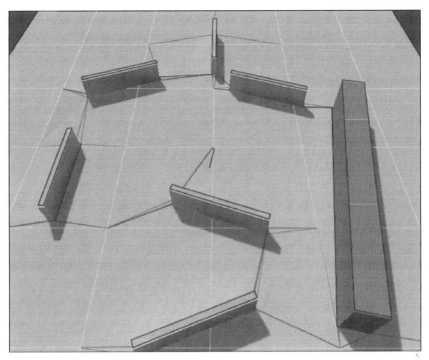

The navigation mesh baked

Using the NavMesh agent

We're pretty much done with setting up our super simple scene. Now, let's add some AI agents to see if it works. We'll use our tank model here, but if you're working with your own scene and don't have this model, you can just put a cube or a sphere entity as an agent. It'll work the same way.

The tank entity

The next step is to add the **NavMesh Agent** component to our tank entity. This component makes pathfinding really easy. We don't need to deal with pathfinding algorithms directly anymore as Unity handles this for us in the background. By just setting the destination property of the component during runtime, our AI agent will automatically find the path itself.

Navigate to **Component** | **Navigation** | **Nav Mesh Agent** to add this component.

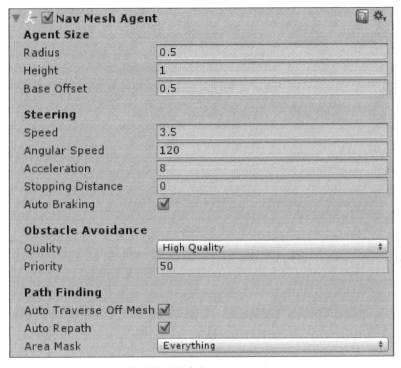

The Nav Mesh Agent properties

 Unity reference for the **NavMesh Agent** component can be found at `http://docs.unity3d.com/Documentation/Components/class-NavMeshAgent.html`.

Setting a destination

Now that we've set up our AI agent, we need a way to tell this agent where to go and update the destination of our tanks to the mouse-click position.

So, let's add a sphere entity to be used as a marker object and then attach the following `Target.cs` script to an empty game object. Drag-and-drop this sphere entity onto this script's `targetMarker` transform property in the inspector.

The Target class

This is a simple class that does three things:

- Gets the mouse-click position using a ray
- Updates the marker position
- Updates the destination property of all the NavMesh agents

The following lines show the code present in this class:

```
using UnityEngine;
using System.Collections;

public class Target : MonoBehaviour {
  private NavMeshAgent[] navAgents;
  public Transform targetMarker;

  void Start() {
    navAgents = FindObjectsOfType(typeof(NavMeshAgent)) as
        NavMeshAgent[];
  }

  void UpdateTargets(Vector3 targetPosition) {
    foreach (NavMeshAgent agent in navAgents) {
      agent.destination = targetPosition;
    }
  }

  void Update() {
    int button = 0;

    //Get the point of the hit position when the mouse is
    //being clicked
    if(Input.GetMouseButtonDown(button)) {
      Ray ray = Camera.main.ScreenPointToRay(
          Input.mousePosition);

      RaycastHit hitInfo;

      if (Physics.Raycast(ray.origin, ray.direction,
          out hitInfo)) {
        Vector3 targetPosition = hitInfo.point;
        UpdateTargets(targetPosition);
        targetMarker.position = targetPosition +
```

```
        new Vector3(0,5,0);
    }
  }
}
}
```

At the start of the game, we look for all the `NavMeshAgent` type entities in our game and store them in our reference `NavMeshAgent` array. Whenever there's a mouse-click event, we do a simple raycast to determine the first objects that collide with our ray. If the ray hits any object, we update the position of our marker and update each NavMesh agent's destination by setting the destination property with the new position. We'll be using this script throughout this chapter to tell the destination position for our AI agents.

Now, test run the scene and click on a point where you want your tanks to go. The tanks should come as close as possible to that point while avoiding the static obstacles like walls.

Testing slopes

Let's build a scene with some slopes like this:

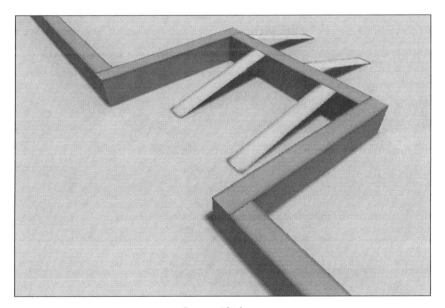

Scene with slopes

One important thing to note is that the slopes and the wall should be in contact with each other. Objects need to be perfectly connected when creating such joints in the scene with the purpose of generating a NavMesh later, otherwise, there'll be gaps in NavMesh and the agents will not be able to find the path anymore. For now, make sure to connect the slope properly.

A well-connected slope

Next, we can adjust the `Max Slope` property in the **Navigation** window's **Bake** tab according to the level of slope in our scenes that we want to allow agents to travel. We'll use `45` degrees here. If your slopes are steeper than this, you can use a higher `Max Slope` value.

Bake the scene, and you should have a NavMesh generated like this:

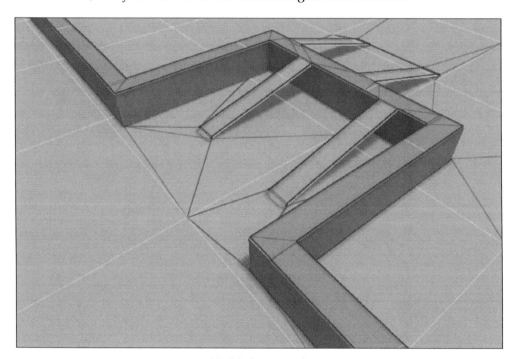

NavMesh generated

Next, we'll place some tanks with the **NavMesh Agent** component. Create a new cube object to be used as a target reference position. We'll be using our previous `Target.cs` script to update the destination property of our AI agent. Test run the scene, and you should have your AI agents crossing the slopes to reach the target.

Exploring areas

In games with complex environments, we usually have some areas that are harder to travel in than others, such as a pond or lake compared to crossing a bridge. Even though it could be the shortest path to target by crossing the pond directly, we would want our agents to choose the bridge as it makes more sense. In other words, we want to make crossing the pond to be more navigationally expensive than using the bridge. In this section, we'll look at NavMesh areas, a way to define different layers with different navigation cost values.

We're going to build a scene, as shown in the following screenshot:

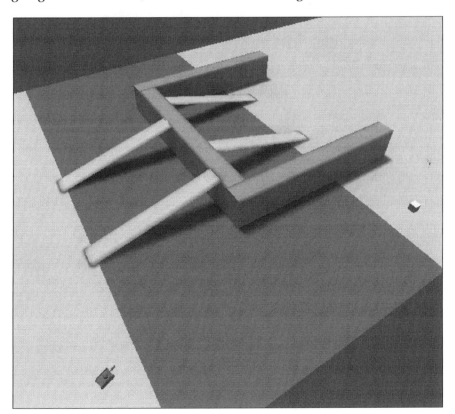

Scene with layers

There'll be three planes to represent two ground planes connected with a bridge-like structure and a water plane between them. As you can see, it's the shortest path for our tank to cross over the water plane to reach our cube target, but we want our AI agents to choose the bridge if possible and to cross the water plane only if absolutely necessary, such as when the target object is on the water plane.

The scene hierarchy can be seen in the following screenshot. Our game level is composed of planes, slopes, and walls. We've a tank entity and a destination cube with the `Target.cs` script attached.

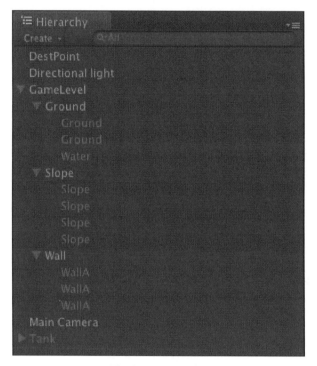

The Scene Hierarchy

As we saw earlier, NavMesh areas can be edited in the **Areas** tab of the **Navigation** window.

Unity comes with three default layers—Default, Not Walkable, and Jump—each with potentially different cost values. Let's add a new layer called Water and give it a cost of 5.

Next, select the water plane. Go to the **Navigation** window and under the **Object** tab, set **Navigation Area** to **Water**.

The Water area

Bake the NavMesh for the scene and run it to test it. You should see that the AI agents now choose the slope rather than going through the plane marked as the water layer because it's more expensive to choose this path. Try experimenting with placing the target object at different points in the water plane. You will see that the AI agents will sometimes swim back to the shore and take the bridge rather than trying to swim all the way across the water.

Making sense of Off Mesh Links

Sometimes, there could be some gaps inside the scene that can make the navigation meshes disconnected. For example, our agents will not be able to find the path if our slopes are not connected to the walls in our previous examples. Or, we could have set up points where our agents could jump off the wall and onto the plane below. Unity has a feature called **Off Mesh Links** to connect such gaps. Off Mesh Links can either be set up manually or generated automatically by Unity's NavMesh generator.

Here's the example scene that we're going to build in this example. As you can see, there's a small gap between the two planes. Let's see how to connect these two planes using Off Mesh Links.

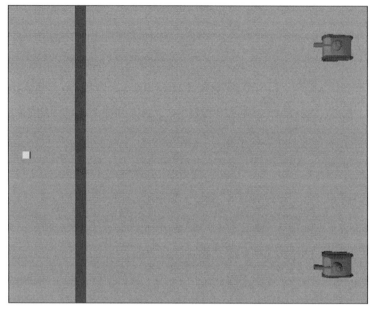

Scene with Off Mesh Links

Using the generated Off Mesh Links

Firstly, we'll use the autogenerated Off Mesh Links to connect the two planes. The first thing to do is to mark these two planes as the **Off Mesh Link Generation** static in the property inspector, as shown in the following screenshot:

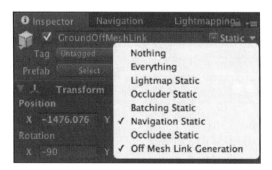

Off Mesh Link Generation static

You can set the distance threshold to autogenerate Off Mesh Links in the **Bake** tab of the **Navigation** window as seen earlier.

Click on **Bake**, and you should have Off Mesh Links connecting two planes like this:

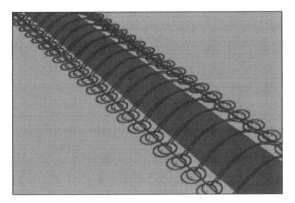

Generated Off Mesh Links

Now our AI agents can traverse and find the path across both planes. Agents will be essentially teleported to the other plane once they have reached the edge of the plane and found the Off Mesh Link. Unless having a teleporting agent is what you want, it might be a good idea to place a bridge to allow the agent to cross.

Setting the manual Off Mesh Links

If we don't want to generate Off Mesh Links along the edge, and want to force the agents to come to a certain point to be teleported to another plane, we can also manually set up the Off Mesh Links. Here's how:

The manual Off Mesh Links setup

This is our scene with a significant gap between two planes. We placed two pairs of sphere entities on both sides of the plane. Choose a sphere, and add an Off Mesh Link by navigating to **Component | Navigation | Off Mesh Link**. We only need to add this component on one sphere. Next, drag-and-drop the first sphere to the **Start** property, and the other sphere to the **End** property.

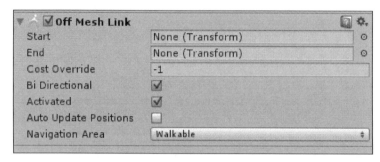

The Off Mesh Link component

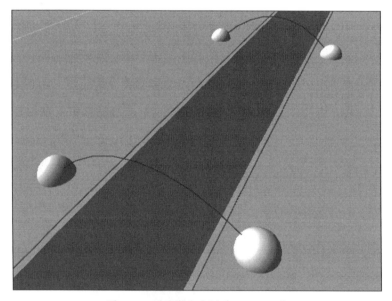

The manual Off Mesh Links generated

Go to the **Navigation** window and bake the scene. The planes are now connected with the manual Off Mesh Links that can be used by AI agents to traverse even though there's a gap.

Summary

You could say we navigated through quite a bit of content in this chapter. We started with a basic waypoint-based system, then learned how to implement our own simple A* Pathfinding system, and finally moved onto Unity's built-in navigation system. While many would opt to go with the simplicity of Unity's NavMesh system, others may find the granular control of a custom A* implementation more appealing. What is most important, however, is understanding when and how to use these different systems.

Furthermore, without even realizing it, we saw how these systems can integrate with other concepts we learned earlier in the book.

In the next chapter, *Flocks and Crowds*, we'll expand on these concepts and learn how we can simulate entire groups of agents moving in unison in a believable and performant fashion.

5
Flocks and Crowds

Flocks and crowds are other essential concepts we'll be exploring in this book. Luckily, flocks are very simple to implement, and they add a fairly extraordinary amount of realism to your simulation in just a few lines of code. Crowds can be a bit more complex, but we'll be exploring some of the powerful tools that come bundled with Unity to get the job done. In this chapter, we'll cover the following topics:

- Learning the history of flocks and herds
- Understanding the concepts behind flocks
- Flocking using the Unity concepts
- Flocking using the traditional algorithm
- Using realistic crowds

Learning the origins of flocks

The flocking algorithm dates all the way back to the mid-80s. It was first developed by Craig Reynolds, who developed it for its use in films, the most famous adaptation of the technology being the swarm of bats in *Batman Returns* in 1992, for which he won an Oscar. Since then, the use of the flocking algorithm has expanded beyond the world of film into various fields from games to scientific research. Despite being highly efficient and accurate, the algorithm is also very simple to understand and implement.

Understanding the concepts behind flocks and crowds

As with previous concepts, it's easiest to understand flocks and herds by relating them to the real-life behaviors they model. As simple as it sounds, these concepts describe a group of objects, or boids, as they are called in artificial intelligence lingo, moving together as a group. The flocking algorithm gets its name from the behavior birds exhibit in nature, where a group of birds follow one another toward a common destination, keeping a mostly fixed distance from each other. The emphasis here is on the group. We've explored how singular agents can move and make decisions on their own, but flocks are a relatively computationally efficient way of simulating large groups of agents moving in unison while modeling unique movement in each boid that doesn't rely on randomness or predefined paths.

We'll implement two variations of flocking in this chapter. The first one will be based on a sample flocking behavior found in a demo project called Tropical Paradise Island. This demo came with Unity in Version 2.0, but has been removed since Unity 3.0. For our first example, we'll salvage this code and adapt it to our Unity 5 project. The second variation will be based on Craig Reynold's flocking algorithm. Along the way, you'll notice some differences and similarities, but there are three basic concepts that define how a flock works, and these concepts have been around since the algorithm's introduction in the 80s:

- **Separation**: This means to maintain a distance with other neighbors in the flock to avoid collision. The following diagram illustrates this concept:

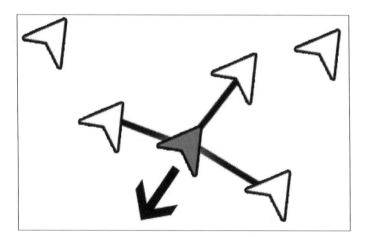

Here, the middle boid is shown moving in a direction away from the rest of the boids, without changing its heading

- **Alignment**: This means to move in the same direction as the flock, and with the same velocity. The following figure illustrates this concept:

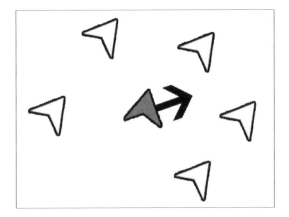

Here, the boid in the middle is shown changing its heading toward the arrow to match the heading of the boids around it

- **Cohesion**: This means to maintain a minimum distance with the flock's center. The following figure illustrates this concept:

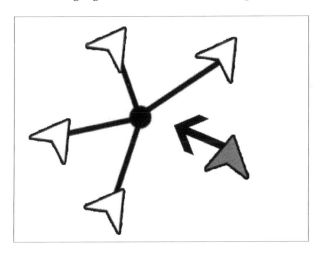

Here, the boid to the right of the rest moves in the direction of the arrow to be within the minimum distance to its nearest group of boids

Flocking using Unity's samples

In this section, we'll create our own scene with flocks of objects and implement the flocking behavior in C#. There are two main components in this example: the individual boid behavior and a main controller to maintain and lead the crowd.

Our scene hierarchy is shown in the following screenshot:

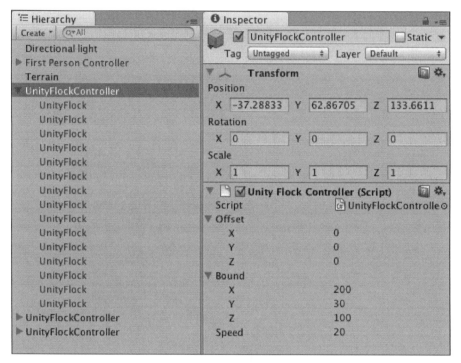

The scene hierarchy

As you can see, we have several boid entities, UnityFlock, under a controller named UnityFlockController. The UnityFlock entities are individual boid objects and they'll reference to their parent UnityFlockController entity to use it as a leader. The UnityFlockController entity will update the next destination point randomly once it reaches the current destination point.

The UnityFlock prefab is a prefab with just a cube mesh and a UnityFlock script. We can use any other mesh representation for this prefab to represent something more interesting, like birds.

Mimicking individual behavior

Boid is a term, coined by Craig Reynold, that refers to a bird-like object. We'll use this term to describe each individual object in our flock. Now let's implement our boid behavior. You can find the following script in `UnityFlock.cs`, and this is the behavior that controls each boid in our flock.

The code in the `UnityFlock.cs` file is as follows:

```
using UnityEngine;
using System.Collections;

public class UnityFlock : MonoBehaviour {
    public float minSpeed = 20.0f;
    public float turnSpeed = 20.0f;
    public float randomFreq = 20.0f;
    public float randomForce = 20.0f;

    //alignment variables
    public float toOriginForce = 50.0f;
    public float toOriginRange = 100.0f;

    public float gravity = 2.0f;

    //seperation variables
    public float avoidanceRadius = 50.0f;
    public float avoidanceForce = 20.0f;

    //cohesion variables
    public float followVelocity = 4.0f;
    public float followRadius = 40.0f;

    //these variables control the movement of the boid
    private Transform origin;
    private Vector3 velocity;
    private Vector3 normalizedVelocity;
    private Vector3 randomPush;
    private Vector3 originPush;
    private Transform[] objects;
    private UnityFlock[] otherFlocks;
    private Transform transformComponent;
```

We declare the input values for our algorithm that can be set up and customized from the editor. First, we define the minimum movement speed, minSpeed, and rotation speed, turnSpeed, for our boid. The randomFreq value is used to determine how many times we want to update the randomPush value based on the randomForce value. This force creates a randomly increased and decreased velocity and makes the flock movement look more realistic.

The toOriginRange value specifies how spread out we want our flock to be. We also use toOriginForce to keep the boids in range and maintain a distance with the flock's origin. Basically, these are the properties to deal with the alignment rule of our flocking algorithm. The avoidanceRadius and avoidanceForce properties are used to maintain a minimum distance between individual boids. These are the properties that apply the separation rule to our flock.

The followRadius and followVelocity values are used to keep a minimum distance with the leader or the origin of the flock. They are used to comply with the cohesion rule of the flocking algorithm.

The origin object will be the parent object to control the whole group of flocking objects. Our boid needs to know about the other boids in the flock. So, we use the objects and otherFlocks properties to store the neighboring boids' information.

The following is the initialization method for our boid:

```
void Start () {
   randomFreq = 1.0f / randomFreq;

   //Assign the parent as origin
   origin = transform.parent;

   //Flock transform
   transformComponent = transform;

   //Temporary components
   Component[] tempFlocks= null;

   //Get all the unity flock components from the parent
   //transform in the group
   if (transform.parent) {
```

```
        tempFlocks = transform.parent.GetComponentsInChildren
            <UnityFlock>();
    }

    //Assign and store all the flock objects in this group
    objects = new Transform[tempFlocks.Length];
    otherFlocks = new UnityFlock[tempFlocks.Length];

    for (int i = 0;i<tempFlocks.Length;i++) {
        objects[i] = tempFlocks[i].transform;
        otherFlocks[i] = (UnityFlock)tempFlocks[i];
    }

    //Null Parent as the flock leader will be
    //UnityFlockController object
    transform.parent = null;

    //Calculate random push depends on the random frequency
//provided
    StartCoroutine(UpdateRandom());
    }
```

We set the parent of the object of our boid as `origin`; it means that this will be the controller object to follow generally. Then, we grab all the other boids in the group and store them in our own variables for later references.

The `StartCoroutine` method starts the `UpdateRandom()` method as a co-routine:

```
    IEnumerator UpdateRandom() {
      while (true) {
        randomPush = Random.insideUnitSphere * randomForce;
        yield return new WaitForSeconds(randomFreq +
            Random.Range(-randomFreq / 2.0f, randomFreq / 2.0f));
      }
    }
```

The `UpdateRandom()` method updates the `randomPush` value throughout the game with an interval based on `randomFreq`. The `Random.insideUnitSphere` part returns a `Vector3` object with random *x*, *y*, and *z* values within a sphere with a radius of the `randomForce` value. Then, we wait for a certain random amount of time before resuming the `while(true)` loop to update the `randomPush` value again.

Now, here's our boid behavior's `Update()` method that helps our boid entity comply with the three rules of the flocking algorithm:

```
void Update () {
  //Internal variables
  float speed = velocity.magnitude;
  Vector3 avgVelocity = Vector3.zero;
  Vector3 avgPosition = Vector3.zero;
  float count = 0;
  float f = 0.0f;
  float d = 0.0f;
  Vector3 myPosition = transformComponent.position;
  Vector3 forceV;
  Vector3 toAvg;
  Vector3 wantedVel;

  for (int i = 0;i<objects.Length;i++){
    Transform transform= objects[i];
    if (transform != transformComponent) {
      Vector3 otherPosition = transform.position;

      // Average position to calculate cohesion
      avgPosition += otherPosition;
      count++;

      //Directional vector from other flock to this flock
      forceV = myPosition - otherPosition;

      //Magnitude of that directional vector(Length)
      d= forceV.magnitude;

      //Add push value if the magnitude, the length of the
      //vector, is less than followRadius to the leader
      if (d < followRadius) {
        //calculate the velocity, the speed of the object, based
         //on the avoidance distance between flocks if the
        //current magnitude is less than the specified
        //avoidance radius
        if (d < avoidanceRadius) {
          f = 1.0f - (d / avoidanceRadius);
```

```
        if (d > 0) avgVelocity +=
            (forceV / d) * f * avoidanceForce;
    }

    //just keep the current distance with the leader
    f = d / followRadius;
    UnityFlock tempOtherFlock = otherFlocks[i];
    //we normalize the tempOtherFlock velocity vector to get
    //the direction of movement, then we set a new velocity
    avgVelocity += tempOtherFlock.normalizedVelocity * f *
        followVelocity;
    }
  }
}
```

The preceding code implements the separation rule. First, we check the distance between the current boid and the other boids and update the velocity accordingly, as explained in the comments.

Next, we calculate the average velocity of the flock by dividing the current velocity with the number of boids in the flock:

```
if (count > 0) {
  //Calculate the average flock velocity(Alignment)
  avgVelocity /= count;

  //Calculate Center value of the flock(Cohesion)
  toAvg = (avgPosition / count) - myPosition;
}
else {
  toAvg = Vector3.zero;
}

//Directional Vector to the leader
forceV = origin.position -  myPosition;
d = forceV.magnitude;
f = d / toOriginRange;

//Calculate the velocity of the flock to the leader
if (d > 0) //if this void is not at the center of the flock
```

```
        originPush = (forceV / d) * f * toOriginForce;

    if (speed < minSpeed && speed > 0) {
      velocity = (velocity / speed) * minSpeed;
    }

    wantedVel = velocity;

    //Calculate final velocity
    wantedVel -= wantedVel *  Time.deltaTime;
    wantedVel += randomPush * Time.deltaTime;
    wantedVel += originPush * Time.deltaTime;
    wantedVel += avgVelocity * Time.deltaTime;
    wantedVel += toAvg.normalized * gravity * Time.deltaTime;

    //Final Velocity to rotate the flock into
    velocity = Vector3.RotateTowards(velocity, wantedVel,
        turnSpeed * Time.deltaTime, 100.00f);

    transformComponent.rotation =
  Quaternion.LookRotation(velocity);

    //Move the flock based on the calculated velocity
    transformComponent.Translate(velocity * Time.deltaTime,
        Space.World);

    //normalise the velocity
    normalizedVelocity = velocity.normalized;
    }
  }
```

Finally, we add up all the factors such as randomPush, originPush, and avgVelocity to calculate our final target velocity, wantedVel. We also update our current velocity to wantedVel with linear interpolation using the Vector3. RotateTowards method. Then, we move our boid based on the new velocity using the Translate() method.

Next, we create a cube mesh and add this `UnityFlock` script to it, and make it a prefab, as shown in the following screenshot:

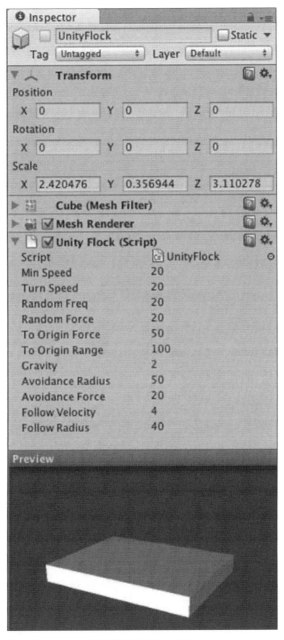

The Unity flock prefab

Creating the controller

Now it is time to create the controller class. This class updates its own position so that the other individual boid objects know where to go. This object is referenced in the `origin` variable in the preceding `UnityFlock` script.

The code in the `UnityFlockController.cs` file is as follows:

```
using UnityEngine;
using System.Collections;

public class UnityFlockController : MonoBehaviour {
  public Vector3 offset;
  public Vector3 bound;
  public float speed = 100.0f;

  private Vector3 initialPosition;
  private Vector3 nextMovementPoint;

  // Use this for initialization
  void Start () {
    initialPosition = transform.position;
    CalculateNextMovementPoint();
  }

  // Update is called once per frame
  void Update () {
    transform.Translate(Vector3.forward * speed * Time.deltaTime);
    transform.rotation = Quaternion.Slerp(transform.rotation,
        Quaternion.LookRotation(nextMovementPoint -
        transform.position), 1.0f * Time.deltaTime);

    if (Vector3.Distance(nextMovementPoint,
        transform.position) <= 10.0f)
        CalculateNextMovementPoint();
  }
```

In our `Update()` method, we check whether our controller object is near the target destination point. If it is, we update our `nextMovementPoint` variable again with the `CalculateNextMovementPoint()` method we just discussed:

```
void CalculateNextMovementPoint () {
  float posX = Random.Range(initialPosition.x - bound.x,
      initialPosition.x + bound.x);
  float posY = Random.Range(initialPosition.y - bound.y,
```

```
            initialPosition.y + bound.y);
        float posZ = Random.Range(initialPosition.z - bound.z,
            initialPosition.z + bound.z);

        nextMovementPoint = initialPosition + new Vector3(posX,
            posY, posZ);
    }
}
```

The `CalculateNextMovementPoint()` method finds the next random destination position in a range between the current position and the boundary vectors.

Putting it all together, as shown in the previous scene hierarchy screenshot, you should have flocks flying around somewhat realistically:

Flocking using the Unity seagull sample

Using an alternative implementation

Here's a simpler implementation of the flocking algorithm. In this example, we'll create a cube object and place a rigid body on our boids. With Unity's rigid body physics, we can simplify the translation and steering behavior of our boid. To prevent our boids from overlapping each other, we'll add a sphere collider physics component.

We'll have two components in this implementation as well: individual boid behavior and controller behavior. The controller will be the object that the rest of the boids try to follow.

The code in the `Flock.cs` file is as follows:

```csharp
using UnityEngine;
using System.Collections;
using System.Collections.Generic;

public class Flock : MonoBehaviour {
  internal FlockController controller;

  void Update () {
    if (controller) {
      Vector3 relativePos = steer() * Time.deltaTime;

      if (relativePos != Vector3.zero)
        rigidbody.velocity = relativePos;

      // enforce minimum and maximum speeds for the boids
      float speed = rigidbody.velocity.magnitude;
      if (speed > controller.maxVelocity) {
        rigidbody.velocity = rigidbody.velocity.normalized *
          controller.maxVelocity;
      }
      else if (speed < controller.minVelocity) {
        rigidbody.velocity = rigidbody.velocity.normalized *
            controller.minVelocity;
      }
    }
  }
```

The `FlockController` will be created in a moment. In our `Update()` method, we calculate the velocity for our boid using the following `steer()` method and apply it to its rigid body velocity. Next, we check the current speed of our rigid body component to verify whether it's in the range of our controller's maximum and minimum velocity limits. If not, we cap the velocity at the preset range:

```
private Vector3 steer () {
  Vector3 center = controller.flockCenter -
      transform.localPosition;  // cohesion

  Vector3 velocity = controller.flockVelocity -
      rigidbody.velocity;  // alignment

  Vector3 follow = controller.target.localPosition -
      transform.localPosition;  // follow leader

  Vector3 separation = Vector3.zero;

  foreach (Flock flock in controller.flockList) {
    if (flock != this) {
      Vector3 relativePos = transform.localPosition -
          flock.transform.localPosition;

      separation += relativePos / (relativePos.sqrMagnitude);
    }
  }

  // randomize
  Vector3 randomize = new Vector3( (Random.value * 2) - 1,
      (Random.value * 2) - 1, (Random.value * 2) - 1);

  randomize.Normalize();

  return (controller.centerWeight * center +
      controller.velocityWeight * velocity +
      controller.separationWeight * separation +
      controller.followWeight * follow +
      controller.randomizeWeight * randomize);
  }
}
```

The `steer()` method implements separation, cohesion, and alignment, and follows the leader rules of the flocking algorithm. Then, we sum up all the factors together with a random weight value. With this `Flock` script together with rigid body and sphere collider components, we create a `Flock` prefab, as shown in the following screenshot:

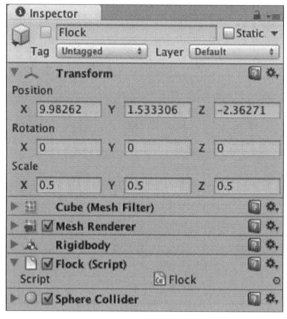

The Flock

Implementing the FlockController

The `FlockController` is a simple behavior to generate the boids at runtime and update the center as well as the average velocity of the flock.

The code in the `FlockController.cs` file is as follows:

```
using UnityEngine;
using System.Collections;
using System.Collections.Generic;

public class FlockController : MonoBehaviour {
  public float minVelocity = 1;  //Min Velocity
  public float maxVelocity = 8;  //Max Flock speed
  public int flockSize = 20;  //Number of flocks in the group

  //How far the boids should stick to the center (the more
```

```
//weight stick closer to the center)
public float centerWeight = 1;

public float velocityWeight = 1;   //Alignment behavior

//How far each boid should be separated within the flock
public float separationWeight = 1;

//How close each boid should follow to the leader (the more
//weight make the closer follow)
public float followWeight = 1;

//Additional Random Noise
public float randomizeWeight = 1;

public Flock prefab;
public Transform target;

//Center position of the flock in the group
internal Vector3 flockCenter;
internal Vector3 flockVelocity;   //Average Velocity

public ArrayList flockList = new ArrayList();

void Start () {
  for (int i = 0; i < flockSize; i++) {
    Flock flock = Instantiate(prefab, transform.position,
        transform.rotation) as Flock;
    flock.transform.parent = transform;
    flock.controller = this;
    flockList.Add(flock);
  }
}
```

We declare all the properties to implement the flocking algorithm and then start with the generation of the boid objects based on the flock size input. We set up the controller class and parent transform object as we did last time. Then, we add the created boid object in our ArrayList function. The target variable accepts an entity to be used as a moving leader. We'll create a sphere entity as a moving target leader for our flock:

```
void Update () {
  //Calculate the Center and Velocity of the whole flock group
  Vector3 center = Vector3.zero;
```

```
    Vector3 velocity = Vector3.zero;

    foreach (Flock flock in flockList) {
      center += flock.transform.localPosition;
      velocity += flock.rigidbody.velocity;
    }

    flockCenter = center / flockSize;
    flockVelocity = velocity / flockSize;
  }
}
```

In our `Update()` method, we keep updating the average center and velocity of the flock. These are the values referenced from our boid object and they are used to adjust the cohesion and alignment properties with the controller.

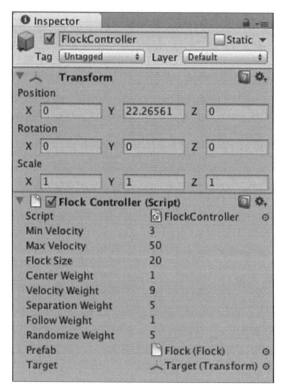

The Flock controller

The following is our `Target` entity with the `TargetMovement` script, which we will create in a moment. The movement script is the same as what we saw in our previous Unity sample controller's movement script:

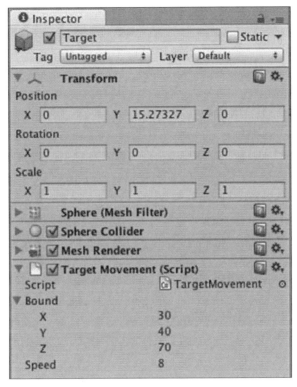

The Target entity with the TargetMovement script

Here is how our `TargetMovement` script works. We pick a random point nearby for the target to move to. When we get close to that point, we pick a new point. The boids will then follow the target.

The code in the `TargetMovement.cs` file is as follows:

```csharp
using UnityEngine;
using System.Collections;

public class TargetMovement : MonoBehaviour {
  //Move target around circle with tangential speed
  public Vector3 bound;
  public float speed = 100.0f;

  private Vector3 initialPosition;
  private Vector3 nextMovementPoint;

  void Start () {
    initialPosition = transform.position;
    CalculateNextMovementPoint();
  }
  void CalculateNextMovementPoint () {
    float posX = Random.Range(initialPosition.x = bound.x,
        initialPosition.x+bound.x);
    float posY = Random.Range(initialPosition.y = bound.y,
        initialPosition.y+bound.y);
    float posZ = Random.Range(initialPosition.z = bound.z,
        initialPosition.z+bound.z);

    nextMovementPoint = initialPosition+
        new Vector3(posX, posY, posZ);
  }
  void Update () {
    transform.Translate(Vector3.forward * speed * Time.deltaTime);
    transform.rotation = Quaternion.Slerp(transform.rotation,
        Quaternion.LookRotation(nextMovementPoint -
        transform.position), 1.0f * Time.deltaTime);

    if (Vector3.Distance(nextMovementPoint, transform.position)
        <= 10.0f) CalculateNextMovementPoint();
  }
}
```

After we put everything together, we should have nice flocking boids flying around in our scene, chasing the target:

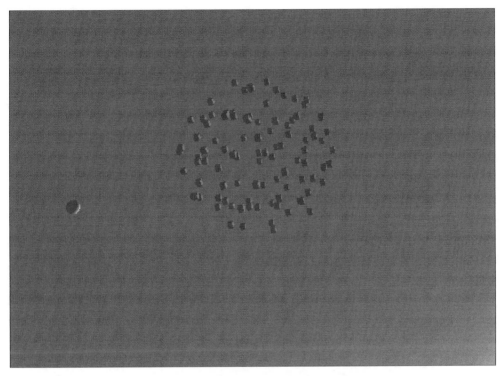

Flocking with Craig Reynold's algorithm

Using crowds

Crowd simulations are far less cut and dry. There really isn't any one way to implement them in a general sense. While not a strict restriction, the term generally refers to simulating crowds of humanoid agents navigating an area while avoiding each other and the environment. Like flocks, the use of crowd simulations has been widely used in films. For example, the epic armies battling one another in *Lord of the Rings* were completely procedurally generated using the crowd simulation software Massive, which was created for using it in the film. While the use of crowd algorithms is not as widespread in video games as in films, certain genres rely on the concept more than others. Real-time strategy games often involve armies of characters, moving in unison across the screen.

Implementing a simple crowd simulation

Our implementation will be quick, simple, and effective, and it will focus on using Unity's NavMesh feature. Thankfully, NavMesh will handle much of the heavy lifting for us. Our scene has a simple walking surface with a NavMesh baked onto it, a couple of targets, and two teams of capsules, as shown in the following screenshot:

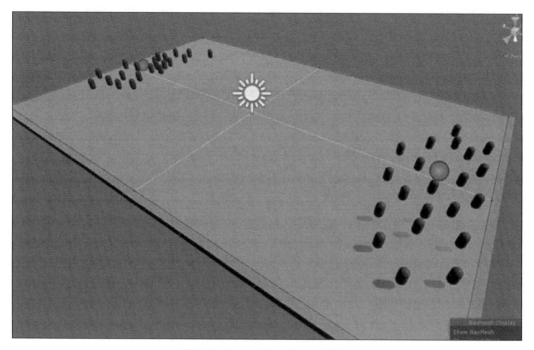

The classic scenario: red versus blue

In the previous screenshot, we can see that our red and blue targets are opposite to their teams—red and blue, respectively. The setup is straightforward. Each capsule has a `CrowdAgent.cs` component attached to it, and when you hit play, each agent will head towards their target while avoiding each other and the oncoming capsules from the opposite team. Once they reach their destination, they will gather around the target.

While the game is running, you can even select a single capsule or a group of them in the editor to see their behavior visualized. As long as you have the navigation window active, you'll be able to see some debugging information about your NavMesh and the agents on it, as you can see in the following screenshot:

It's worth checking this out in the editor to really get an idea of how this looks in motion, but we've labeled a few key elements in the preceding screenshot:

- **1**: This is the destination arrow that points toward the NavMeshAgent destination, which for this little guy is RedTarget. All this arrow cares about is where the destination is, regardless of the direction the agent is facing or moving toward.

- **2**: This arrow is the heading arrow. It shows the actual direction the agent is moving in. The direction of the agent takes into account several factors, including the position of its neighbors, space on the NavMesh, and the destination.

- **3**: This debug menu allows you to show a few different things. In our case, we enabled **Show Avoidance** and **Show Neighbours**.

- **4**: Speaking of avoidance, this cluster of squares, ranging from dark to light and floating over the agents, represents the areas to avoid between our agent and the destination. The darker squares indicate areas that are densely populated by other agents or blocked by the environment, while the lighter-white squares indicate areas that are safe to walk through. Of course, this is a dynamic display, so watch it change as you play in the editor.

Using the CrowdAgent component

The CrowdAgent component is incredibly simple, but gets the job done. As mentioned earlier, Unity does most of the heavy lifting for us. The following code gives our CrowdAgent a destination:

```
using UnityEngine;
using System.Collections;

[RequireComponent(typeof(NavMeshAgent))]
public class CrowdAgent : MonoBehaviour {

    public Transform target;

    private NavMeshAgent agent;

    void Start () {
        agent = GetComponent<NavMeshAgent>();
        agent.speed = Random.Range(4.0f, 5.0f);
        agent.SetDestination(target.position);
    }
}
```

The script requires a component of type `NavMeshAgent`, which it assigns to the `agent` variable on `Start()`. We then set its speed randomly between two values for some added effect. Lastly, we set its destination to be the position of the target marker. The target marker is assigned via the inspector, as you can see in the following screenshot:

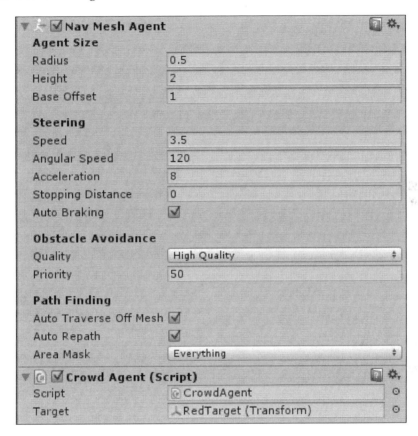

The preceding screenshot illustrates a red capsule as it has **RedTarget (Transform)** set as its **Target**.

Adding some fun obstacles

Without having to do anything else in our code, we can make a few changes to our scene layout and enable a few components provided by Unity to dramatically alter the behavior of our agents. In our CrowdsObstacles scene, we've added a few walls to the environment, creating a maze-like layout for our red and blue teams of capsules to traverse, as you can see in the following screenshot:

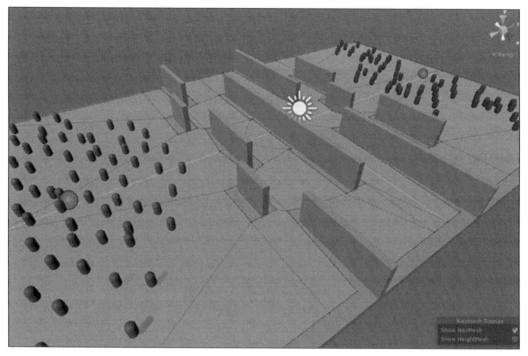

Let the game begin!

The fun part about this example is that because of the randomized speed of each agent, the results will be totally different each time. As the agents move through the environment, they'll be blocked by teammates or opposing agents and will be forced to re-route and find the quickest route to their target. Of course, this concept is not new to us, as we saw NavMeshAgent avoiding obstacles in *Chapter 4, Finding Your Way*, except that we have many, many more agents in this scenario. To add a bit more fun to the example, we've also added a simple up-down animation to one of the walls and a NavMeshObstacle component, which looks something like this:

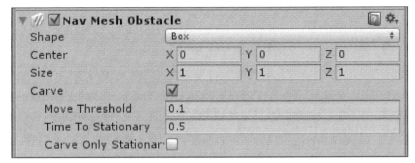

Nav Mesh Obstacle looks a bit different in Unity 5

Note that our obstacle does not need to be set to **Static** when we are using this component. Our obstacle is mostly box-like, so we leave the default **Shape** setting as **Box** (**Capsule** is another choice). The **Size** and **Center** options let us move the outline of our shape around and resize it, but the default settings fit our shape perfectly, which is what we want, so let's leave that alone. The next option **Carve** is important. It essentially does exactly what it says; it carves a space out of the NavMesh, as shown in the following screenshot:

The sane obstacle at two different points of its up-down animation

The left screenshot shows the space carved out when the obstacle is on the surface, while the NavMesh is connected in the right screenshot when the obstacle is raised off the surface. We can leave **Time to Stationary** and **Move Threshold** as they are, but we do want to make sure that **Carve Only Stationary** is turned off. This is because our obstacle is moving, and if we didn't tick this box, it would not carve out the space from the NavMesh, and our agents would be trying to move through the obstacle whether it was up or down, which is not the behavior we are after in this case.

As the obstacle moves up and down and the mesh is carved out and reconnected, you'll notice the agents changing their heading. With the navigation debug options enabled, we can also see a very interesting visualization of everything going on with our agents at any given moment. It may seem a bit cruel to mess with our poor agents like this, but we're doing it for science!

The following screenshot gives us a glimpse into the chaos and disorder we're subjecting our poor agents to:

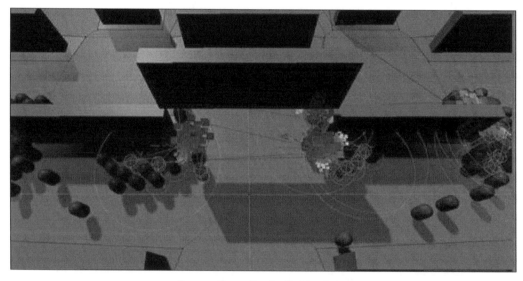

I'm secretly rooting for the blue team

Summary

In this chapter, we learned how to implement flocking behavior in two ways. First, we examined, dissected, and learned how to implement a flocking algorithm based on Unity's Tropical Island Demo project. Next, we implemented it using rigid body to control the boid's movement and sphere collider to avoid collision with other boids. We applied our flocking behavior to the flying objects, but you can apply the techniques in these examples to implement other character behaviors such as fish shoaling, insects swarming, or land animals herding. You'll only have to implement different leader movement behaviors such as limiting movement along the y axis for characters that can't move up and down. For a 2D game, we would just freeze the y position. For 2D movement along uneven terrain, we would have to modify our script to not put any forces in the y direction.

We also took a look at crowd simulation and even implemented our own version of it using Unity's NavMesh system, which we first learned about in *Chapter 4, Finding Your Way*. We learned how to visualize our agents' behavior and decision-making process.

In the next chapter, *Behavior Trees*, we'll look at the behavior tree pattern and learn to implement our own version of it from scratch.

6

Behavior Trees

Behavior trees (BTs) have been gaining popularity among game developers very steadily. Over the last decade, BTs have become the pattern of choice for many AAA studios when it comes to implementing AI for their agents. Games like Halo and Gears of War are among the more famous franchises to make extensive use of BTs. An abundance of computing power in PCs, gaming consoles, and mobile devices has made them a good option for implementing AI in games of all types and scopes.

In this chapter, we will cover the following topics:

- The basics of a behavior tree
- The benefits of using existing behavior tree solutions
- How to implement our own behavior tree framework
- How to implement a basic tree using our framework

Learning the basics of behavior trees

It is called a tree because it is a hierarchical, branching system of nodes with a common parent, known as the root. As you've surely learned from reading this book, by now, behavior trees, too, mimic the real thing they are named after—in this case, trees. If we were to visualize a behavior tree, it would look something like the following figure:

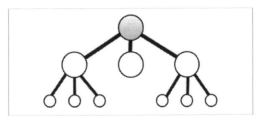

A basic tree structure

Of course, behavior trees can be made up of any number of nodes and children nodes. The nodes at the very end of the hierarchy are referred to as leaf nodes, just like a tree. Nodes can represent behaviors or tests. Unlike state machines, which rely on transition rules to traverse through it, a BT's flow is defined strictly by each node's order within the larger hierarchy. A BT begins evaluating from the top (based on the preceding visualization) of the tree, then continues through each child, which, in turn, runs through each of its children until a condition is met or the leaf node is reached. BTs always begin evaluating from the root node.

Understanding different node types

The names of the different types of nodes may vary depending on who you ask, and even nodes themselves are sometimes referred to as tasks. While the complexity of a tree is dependent entirely upon the needs of the AI, the high-level concepts about how BTs work are fairly easy to understand if we look at each component individually. The following is true for each node regardless of what type of node we're referring to. A node will always return one of the following states:

- **Success**: The condition the node was checking for has been met.

- **Failure**: The condition the node was checking for was not, and will not be met.

- **Running**: The validity of the condition the node is checking for has not been determined. Think of this as our "please wait" state.

Due to the potential complexity of a BT, most implementations are asynchronous, which, at least for Unity, means that evaluating a tree will not block the game from continuing other operations. The evaluation process of the various nodes in a BT can take several frames, if necessary. If you had to evaluate several trees on any number of agents at a time, you can imagine how it would negatively affect the performance of the program to have to wait for each of them to return a true or false to the root node. This is why the "running" state is important.

Defining composite nodes

Composite nodes are called so as they have one or more children. Their state is based entirely upon the result of evaluating its children, and while its children are being evaluated, it will be in a "running" state. There are a couple of composite node types, which are mostly defined by how their children are evaluated:

- **Sequences**: The defining characteristic of a sequence is that the entire sequence of children needs to complete successfully in order for it to evaluate as a success itself. If any of the children at any step of the sequence return false, the sequence itself will report a failure. It is important to note that, in general, sequences are executed from left to right. The following figures show a successful sequence and a failed sequence, respectively:

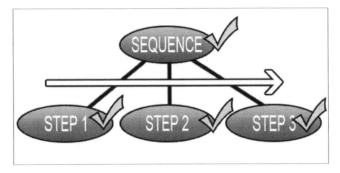

A successful sequence node

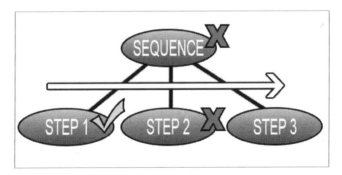

An unsuccessful sequence node

- **Selectors**: By comparison, selectors are much more forgiving parents to their children nodes. If any one of the children nodes in a selector sequence returns true, the selector says, "eh, good enough!" and returns true immediately, without evaluating any more of its children. The only way a selector node will return false is if all of its children are evaluated and none of them return a success.

Of course, each composite node type has its use depending on the situation. You can think of the different types of sequence nodes as "and" and "or" conditionals.

Understanding decorator nodes

The biggest difference between a composite node and a decorator node is that a decorator can have exactly one child and one child only. At first, this may seem unnecessary as you would, in theory, be able to get the same functionality by containing the condition in the node itself rather than relying on its child, but the decorator node is special in that it essentially takes the state returned by the child and evaluates the response based on its own parameters. A decorator can even specify how its children are evaluated and how often they are. These are some common decorator types:

- **Inverter**: Think of the inverter as a NOT modifier. It takes the opposite of the state returned by its child. For example, if the child returns TRUE, the decorator evaluates as FALSE, and vice versa. This is the equivalent of having the ! operator in front of a Boolean in C#.

- **Repeater**: This repeats the evaluation of the child a specified (or infinite) number of times until it evaluates as either TRUE or FALSE as determined by the decorator. For example, you may want to wait indefinitely until a certain condition is met, such as "having enough energy" before a character uses an attack.

- **Limiter**: This simply limits the number of times a node will be evaluated to avoid getting an agent stuck in an awkward infinite behavior loop. This decorator, in contrast to the repeater, can be used to make sure a character only tries to, for example, kick the door open so many times before giving up and trying something else.

Some decorator nodes can be used for debugging and testing your trees. For example:

- **Fake state**: This always evaluates true or false as specified by the decorator. This is very helpful for asserting certain behavior in your agent. You can also have the decorator maintain a fake "running" state indefinitely to see how other agents around it will behave, for example.

- **Breakpoint**: Just like a breakpoint in code, you can have this node fire off logic to notify you via debug logs or other methods that the node has been reached.

These types are not monolithic archetypes that are mutually exclusive. You can combine these types of nodes to suit your needs. Just be careful not to combine too much functionality into one decorator to the point where it may be more efficient or convenient to use a sequence node instead.

Describing the leaf node

We briefly covered leaf nodes earlier in the chapter to make a point about the structure of a BT, but leaf nodes, in reality, can be just about any sort of behavior. They are magical in the sense that they can be used to describe any sort of logic your agent can have. A leaf node can specify a walk function, shoot command, or kick action. It doesn't matter what it does or how you decide to have it evaluate its states, it just has to be the last node in its own hierarchy and return any of the three states a node can return.

Evaluating the existing solutions

The unity asset store is an excellent resource for developers. Not only are you able to purchase art, audio, and other kinds of assets, but it is also populated with a large number of plugins and frameworks. Most relevant to our purposes, there are a number of behavior tree plugins available on the asset store, ranging from free to a few hundred dollars. Most, if not all, provide some sort of GUI to make visualizing and arranging a fairly painless experience.

There are many advantages of going with an off-the-shelf solution from the asset store. Many of the frameworks include advanced functionality such as runtime (and often visual) debugging, robust APIs, serialization, and data-oriented tree support. Many even include sample leaf logic nodes to use in your game, minimizing the amount of coding you have to do to get up and running.

The previous edition of this book, *Unity 4.x Game AI Programming*, focused on developer AngryAnt's Behave plugin, which is currently available as Behave 2 for Unity on the asset store as a paid plugin, which continues to be an excellent choice for your behavior tree needs (and so much more). It is a very robust, performant, and excellently designed framework.

Some other alternatives are Behavior Machine and Behavior Designer, which offer different pricing tiers (Behavior Machine even offers a free edition) and a wide array of useful features. Many other options can be found for free around the Web as both generic C# and Unity-specific implementations. Ultimately, as with any other system, the choice of rolling your own or using an existing solution will depend on your time, budget, and project.

Implementing a basic behavior tree framework

While a fully-fledged implementation of a behavior tree with a GUI and its many node types and variations is outside the scope of this book, we can certainly focus on the core principles to get a solid grasp on what the concepts we've covered in this chapter look similar to in action. Provided with this chapter is the basic framework for a behavior tree. Our example will focus on simple logic to highlight the functionality of the tree rather than muddy up the example with complex game logic. The goal of our example is to make you feel comfortable with what can seem like an intimidating concept in game AI, and give you the necessary tools to build your own tree and expand upon the provided code if you do so.

Implementing a base Node class

There is a base functionality that needs to go into every node. Our simple framework will have all the nodes derived from a base abstract Node.cs class. This class will provide said base functionality or at least the signature to expand upon that functionality:

```
using UnityEngine;
using System.Collections;

[System.Serializable]
public abstract class Node {

    /* Delegate that returns the state of the node.*/
    public delegate NodeStates NodeReturn();

    /* The current state of the node */
    protected NodeStates m_nodeState;

    public NodeStates nodeState {
        get { return m_nodeState; }
    }

    /* The constructor for the node */
    public Node() {}

    /* Implementing classes use this method to evaluate the desired
set of conditions */
    public abstract NodeStates Evaluate();

}
```

The class is fairly simple. Think of `Node.cs` as a blueprint for all the other node types to be built upon. We begin with the `NodeReturn` delegate, which is not implemented in our example, but the next two fields are. However, `m_nodeState` is the state of a node at any given point. As we learned earlier, it will be either FAILURE, SUCCESS, or RUNNING. The `nodeState` value is simply a getter for `m_nodeState` since it is protected and we don't want any other area of the code directly setting `m_nodeState` inadvertently.

Next, we have an empty constructor, for the sake of being explicit, even though it is not being used. Lastly, we have the meat and potatoes of our `Node.cs` class—the `Evaluate()` method. As we'll see in the classes that implement `Node.cs`, `Evaluate` is where the magic happens. It runs the code that determines the state of the node.

Extending nodes to selectors

To create a selector, we simply expand upon the functionality that we described in the `Node.cs` class:

```
using UnityEngine;
using System.Collections;
using System.Collections.Generic;

public class Selector : Node {
    /** The child nodes for this selector */
    protected List<Node> m_nodes = new List<Node>();


    /** The constructor requires a list of child nodes to be
     * passed in*/
    public Selector(List<Node> nodes) {
        m_nodes = nodes;
    }

    /* If any of the children reports a success, the selector will
     * immediately report a success upwards. If all children fail,
     * it will report a failure instead.*/
    public override NodeStates Evaluate() {
        foreach (Node node in m_nodes) {
            switch (node.Evaluate()) {
                case NodeStates.FAILURE:
                    continue;
                case NodeStates.SUCCESS:
                    m_nodeState = NodeStates.SUCCESS;
                    return m_nodeState;
```

```
                case NodeStates.RUNNING:
                    m_nodeState = NodeStates.RUNNING;
                    return m_nodeState;
                default:
                    continue;
            }
        }
        m_nodeState = NodeStates.FAILURE;
        return m_nodeState;
    }
}
```

As we learned earlier in the chapter, selectors are composite nodes; this means that they have one or more child nodes. These child nodes are stored in the m_nodes List<Node> variable. Though it's conceivable that one could extend the functionality of this class to allow adding more child nodes after the class has been instantiated, we initially provide this list via the constructor.

The next portion of the code is a bit more interesting as it shows us a real implementation of the concepts we learned earlier. The Evaluate() method runs through all of its child nodes and evaluates each one individually. As a failure doesn't necessarily mean a failure for the entire selector, if one of the children returns FAILURE, we simply continue onto the next one. Inversely, if any child returns SUCCESS, then we're all set—we can set this node's state accordingly and return that value. If we make it through the entire list of child nodes and none of them have returned SUCCESS, then we can essentially determine that the entire selector has failed and we assign and return a FAILURE state.

Moving on to sequences

Sequences are very similar in their implementation, but as you might have guessed by now, the Evaluate() method behaves differently:

```
using UnityEngine;
using System.Collections;
using System.Collections.Generic;

public class Sequence : Node {
    /** Chiildren nodes that belong to this sequence */
    private List<Node> m_nodes = new List<Node>();

    /** Must provide an initial set of children nodes to work */
    public Sequence(List<Node> nodes) {
        m_nodes = nodes;
```

```
    }

    /* If any child node returns a failure, the entire node fails.
Whence all
     * nodes return a success, the node reports a success. */
    public override NodeStates Evaluate() {
        bool anyChildRunning = false;

        foreach(Node node in m_nodes) {
            switch (node.Evaluate()) {
                case NodeStates.FAILURE:
                    m_nodeState = NodeStates.FAILURE;
                    return m_nodeState;
                case NodeStates.SUCCESS:
                    continue;
                case NodeStates.RUNNING:
                    anyChildRunning = true;
                    continue;
                default:
                    m_nodeState = NodeStates.SUCCESS;
                    return m_nodeState;
            }
        }
        m_nodeState = anyChildRunning ? NodeStates.RUNNING :
NodeStates.SUCCESS;
        return m_nodeState;
    }
}
```

The Evaluate() method in a sequence will need to return true for all the child nodes, and if any one of them fails during the process, the entire sequence fails, which is why we check for FAILURE first and set and report it accordingly. A SUCCESS state simply means we get to live to fight another day, and we continue onto the next child node. If any of the child nodes are determined to be in the RUNNING state, we report that as the state for the node and then the parent node or the logic driving the entire tree can re-evaluate it again.

Implementing a decorator as an inverter

The structure of `Inverter.cs` is a bit different, but it derives from `Node`, just like the rest of the nodes. Let's take a look at the code and spot the differences:

```
using UnityEngine;
using System.Collections;

public class Inverter : Node {
    /* Child node to evaluate */
    private Node m_node;

    public Node node {
        get { return m_node; }
    }

    /* The constructor requires the child node that this inverter
decorator
     * wraps*/
    public Inverter(Node node) {
        m_node = node;
    }

    /* Reports a success if the child fails and
     * a failure if the child succeeds. Running will report
     * as running */
    public override NodeStates Evaluate() {
        switch (m_node.Evaluate()) {
            case NodeStates.FAILURE:
                m_nodeState = NodeStates.SUCCESS;
                return m_nodeState;
            case NodeStates.SUCCESS:
                m_nodeState = NodeStates.FAILURE;
                return m_nodeState;
            case NodeStates.RUNNING:
                m_nodeState = NodeStates.RUNNING;
                return m_nodeState;
        }
        m_nodeState = NodeStates.SUCCESS;
        return m_nodeState;
    }
}
```

As you can see, since a decorator only has one child, we don't have List<Node>, but rather a single node variable, m_node. We pass this node in via the constructor (essentially requiring it), but there is no reason you couldn't modify this code to provide an empty constructor and a method to assign the child node after instantiation.

The Evalute() implementation implements the behavior of an inverter that we described earlier in the chapter — when the child evaluates as SUCCESS, the inverter reports a FAILURE, and when the child evaluates as FAILURE, the inverter reports a SUCCESS. The RUNNING state is reported normally.

Creating a generic action node

Now we arrive at ActionNode.cs, which is a generic leaf node to pass in some logic via a delegate. You are free to implement leaf nodes in any way that fits your logic, as long as it derives from Node. This particular example is equal parts flexible and restrictive. It's flexible in the sense that it allows you to pass in any method matching the delegate signature, but is restrictive for this very reason — it only provides one delegate signature that doesn't take in any arguments:

```
using System;
using UnityEngine;
using System.Collections;

public class ActionNode : Node {
    /* Method signature for the action. */
    public delegate NodeStates ActionNodeDelegate();

    /* The delegate that is called to evaluate this node */
    private ActionNodeDelegate m_action;

    /* Because this node contains no logic itself,
     * the logic must be passed in in the form of
     * a delegate. As the signature states, the action
     * needs to return a NodeStates enum */
    public ActionNode(ActionNodeDelegate action) {
        m_action = action;
    }

    /* Evaluates the node using the passed in delegate and
     * reports the resulting state as appropriate */
    public override NodeStates Evaluate() {
        switch (m_action()) {
            case NodeStates.SUCCESS:
                m_nodeState = NodeStates.SUCCESS;
```

```
                    return m_nodeState;
            case NodeStates.FAILURE:
                m_nodeState = NodeStates.FAILURE;
                return m_nodeState;
            case NodeStates.RUNNING:
                m_nodeState = NodeStates.RUNNING;
                return m_nodeState;
            default:
                m_nodeState = NodeStates.FAILURE;
                return m_nodeState;
            }
        }
    }
```

The key for making this node work is the `m_action` delegate. For those familiar with C++, a delegate in C# can be thought of as a function pointer of sorts. You can also think of a delegate as a variable containing (or more accurately, pointing to) a function. This allows you to set the function to be called at runtime. The constructor requires you to pass in a method matching its signature, and is expecting that method to return a `NodeStates` enum. That method can implement any logic you want as long as these conditions are meant. Unlike other nodes we've implemented, this one doesn't fall through to any state outside of the switch itself, so it defaults to a `FAILURE` state. You may choose to default to a `SUCCESS` or `RUNNING` state, if you so wish, by modifying the default return.

You can easily expand on this class by deriving from it or simply making the changes to it that you need. You can also skip this generic action node altogether and implement one-off versions of specific leaf nodes, but it's good practice to reuse as much code as possible. Just remember to derive from `Node` and implement the required code!

Testing our framework

The framework that we just reviewed is nothing more than this. It provides us with all the functionality we need to make a tree, but we have to make the actual tree ourselves. For the purposes of this book, a somewhat manually constructed tree is provided.

Planning ahead

Before we set up our tree, let's look at what we're trying to accomplish. It is often helpful to visualize a tree before implementing it. Our tree will count up from zero to a specified value. Along the way, it will check whether certain conditions are met for that value and report its state accordingly. The following diagram illustrates the basic hierarchy for our tree:

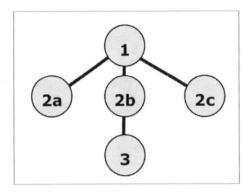

For our tests, we will use a three-tier tree, including the root node:

- **Node 1**: This is our root node. It has children, and we want to be able to return a success if any of the children is a success, so we'll implement it as a selector.

- **Node 2a**: We'll implement this node using an `ActionNode`.

- **Node 2b**: We'll use this node to demonstrate how our inverter works.

- **Node 2c**: We'll run the same `ActionNode` from node 2a again, and see how that affects our tree's evaluation.

- **Node 3**: Node 3 happens to be the lone node in the third tier of the tree. It is the child of the 2b decorator node. This means that if it reports SUCCESS, 2b will report a FAILURE, and vice versa.

At this point, we're still a bit vague on the implementation details, but the preceding diagram will help us to visualize our tree as we implement it in code. Keep it handy for reference as we go through the code.

Examining our scene setup

We've now looked at the basic structure of our tree, and before we jump in and dig into the actual code implementation, let's look at our scene setup. The following screenshot shows our hierarchy; the nodes are highlighted for emphasis:

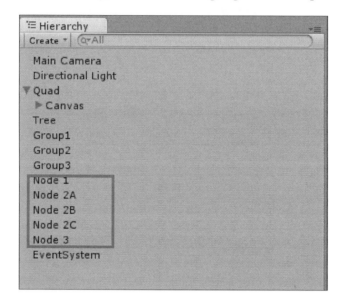

The setup is quite simple. There is a quad with a world-space canvas, which is simply to display some information during the test. The nodes highlighted in the preceding screenshot will be referenced in the code later, and we'll be using them to visualize the status of each individual node. The actual scene looks something like the following screenshot:

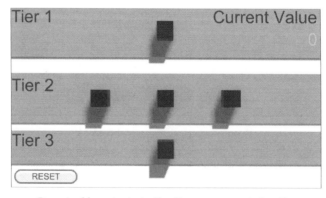

Our actual layout mimics the diagram we created earlier

As you can see, we have one node or box representing each one of the nodes that we laid out in our planning phase. These are referenced in the actual test code and will be changing colors according to the state that is returned.

Exploring the MathTree code

Without further ado, let's have a look at the code driving our test. This is `MathTree.cs`:

```
using UnityEngine;
using UnityEngine.UI;
using System.Collections;
using System.Collections.Generic;

public class MathTree : MonoBehaviour {
    public Color m_evaluating;
    public Color m_succeeded;
    public Color m_failed;

    public Selector m_rootNode;

    public ActionNode m_node2A;
    public Inverter m_node2B;
    public ActionNode m_node2C;
    public ActionNode m_node3;

    public GameObject m_rootNodeBox;
    public GameObject m_node2aBox;
    public GameObject m_node2bBox;
    public GameObject m_node2cBox;
    public GameObject m_node3Box;

    public  int m_targetValue = 20;
    private int m_currentValue = 0;

    [SerializeField]
    private Text m_valueLabel;
```

The first few variables are simply used for debugging. The three color variables are the colors we'll be assigning to our node boxes to visualize their state. By default, RUNNING is yellow, SUCCESS is green, and FAILED is red. This is pretty standard stuff; let's move along.

We then declare our actual nodes. As you can see, m_rootNode is a selector as we mentioned earlier. Notice that we do not assign any of the node variables yet, since we have to pass in some data to their constructors.

We then have the references to the boxes we saw in our scene. These are just GameObjects that we drag-and-drop into the inspector (we'll have a look at that after we inspect the code).

We then have a couple of int values, which will make more sense as we look at the logic, so we'll skip over these. Lastly, we have a unity UI Text variable that will display some values for us during the test.

Let's get into the initialization of our actual nodes:

```
    /* We instantiate our nodes from the bottom up, and assign the
children
      * in that order */
   void Start () {
        /** The deepest-level node is Node 3, which has no children.
*/
        m_node3 = new ActionNode(NotEqualToTarget);

        /** Next up, we create the level 2 nodes. */
        m_node2A = new ActionNode(AddTen);

        /** Node 2B is a selector which has node 3 as a child, so
we'll pass
         * node 3 to the constructor */
        m_node2B = new Inverter(m_node3);

        m_node2C = new ActionNode(AddTen);

        /** Lastly, we have our root node. First, we prepare our list
of children
         * nodes to pass in */
        List<Node> rootChildren = new List<Node>();
        rootChildren.Add(m_node2A);
        rootChildren.Add(m_node2B);
        rootChildren.Add(m_node2C);

        /** Then we create our root node object and pass in the list
*/
        m_rootNode = new Selector(rootChildren);

        m_valueLabel.text = m_currentValue.ToString();

        m_rootNode.Evaluate();

        UpdateBoxes();
    }
```

For the sake of organization, we declare our nodes from the bottom of the tree to the top of the tree, or the root node. We do this because we cannot instantiate a parent without passing in its child nodes, so we have to instantiate the child nodes first. Notice that m_node2A, m_node2C, and m_node3 are action nodes, so we pass in delegates (we'll look at these methods next). Then, m_node2B, being a selector, takes in a node as a child, in this case, m_node3. After we've declared these tiers, we throw all the tier 2 nodes into a list because our tier 1 node, the root node, is a selector that requires a list of children to be instantiated.

After we've instantiated all of our nodes, we kick off the process and begin evaluating our root node using its Evaluate() method. The UpdateBoxes() method simply updates the box game objects that we declared earlier with the appropriate colors; we'll look at that up ahead in this section:

```
private void UpdateBoxes() {
    /** Update root node box */
    if (m_rootNode.nodeState == NodeStates.SUCCESS) {
        SetSucceeded(m_rootNodeBox);
    } else if (m_rootNode.nodeState == NodeStates.FAILURE) {
        SetFailed(m_rootNodeBox);
    }

    /** Update 2A node box */
    if (m_node2A.nodeState == NodeStates.SUCCESS) {
        SetSucceeded(m_node2aBox);
    } else if (m_node2A.nodeState == NodeStates.FAILURE) {
        SetFailed(m_node2aBox);
    }

    /** Update 2B node box */
    if (m_node2B.nodeState == NodeStates.SUCCESS) {
        SetSucceeded(m_node2bBox);
    } else if (m_node2B.nodeState == NodeStates.FAILURE) {
        SetFailed(m_node2bBox);
    }

    /** Update 2C node box */
    if (m_node2C.nodeState == NodeStates.SUCCESS) {
        SetSucceeded(m_node2cBox);
    } else if (m_node2C.nodeState == NodeStates.FAILURE) {
        SetFailed(m_node2cBox);
    }

    /** Update 3 node box */
```

```
        if (m_node3.nodeState == NodeStates.SUCCESS) {
            SetSucceeded(m_node3Box);
        } else if (m_node3.nodeState == NodeStates.FAILURE) {
            SetFailed(m_node3Box);
        }
    }
```

There is not a whole lot to discuss here. Do notice that because we set this tree up manually, we check each node individually and get its nodeState and set the colors using the SetSucceeded and SetFailed methods. Let's move on to the meaty part of the class:

```
private NodeStates NotEqualToTarget() {
        if (m_currentValue != m_targetValue) {
            return NodeStates.SUCCESS;
        } else {
            return NodeStates.FAILURE;
        }
    }


private NodeStates AddTen() {
        m_currentValue += 10;
        m_valueLabel.text = m_currentValue.ToString();
        if (m_currentValue == m_targetValue) {
            return NodeStates.SUCCESS;
        } else {
            return NodeStates.FAILURE;
        }
    }
```

First, we have NotEqualToTarget(), which is the method we passed into our decorator's child action node. We're essentially setting ourselves up for a double negative here, so try to follow along. This method returns a success if the current value is *not* equal to the target value, and returns false otherwise. The parent inverter decorator will then evaluate to the opposite of what this node returns. So, if the value is not equal, the inverter node will fail; otherwise, it will succeed. If you're feeling a bit lost at this point, don't worry. It will all make sense when we see this in action.

The next method is the AddTen() method, which is the method passed into our other two action nodes. It does exactly what the name implies—it adds 10 to our m_currentValue variable, then checks if it's equal to our m_targetValue, and evaluates as SUCCESS if so, and FAILURE, if not.

The last few methods are self-explanatory so we will not go over them.

Executing the test

Now that we have a pretty good idea of how the code works, let's see it in action. First thing first, however. Let's make sure our component is properly setup. Select the **Tree** game object from the hierarchy, and its inspector should look similar to this:

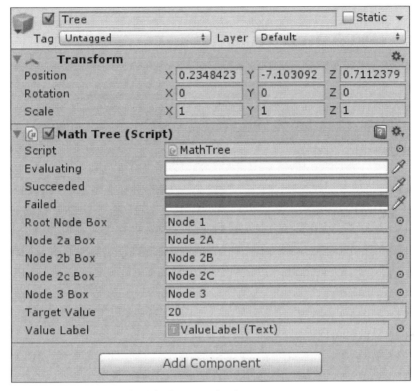

The default settings for the component

As you can see, the state colors and box references have already been assigned for you, as well as the m_valueLabel variable. The m_targetValue variable has also been assigned for you via code. Make sure to leave it at (or set it to) 20 before you hit play. Play the scene, and you'll see your boxes lit up, as shown in the following screenshot:

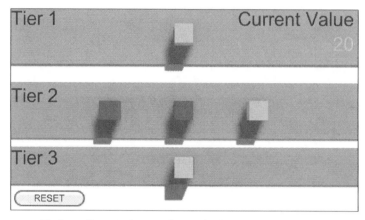

The boxes lit up, indicating the result of each node's evaluation

As we can see, our root node evaluated to SUCCESS, which is what we intended, but let's examine why, one step at a time, starting at tier 2:

- **Node 2A**: We started with m_currentValue at 0, so upon adding 10 to it, it's still not equal to our m_targetValue (20) and it fails. Thus, it is red.

- **Node 2B**: As it evaluates its child, once again, m_currentValue and m_targetValue are not equal. This returns SUCCESS. Then, the inverter logic kicks in and reverses this response so that it reports FAILURE for itself. So, we move on to the last node.

- **Node 2C**: Once again, we add 10 to m_currentValue. It then becomes 20, which is equal to m_targetValue, and evaluates as SUCCESS, so our root node is successful as result.

The test is simple, but it illustrates the concepts clearly. Before we consider the test a success, let's run it one more time, but change m_targetValue first. Set it to 30 in the inspector, as shown in the following screenshot:

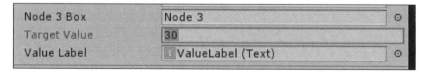

The updated value is highlighted

A small change to be sure, but it will change how the entire tree evaluates. Play the scene again, and we will end up with the set of nodes lit up, as shown in the following screenshot:

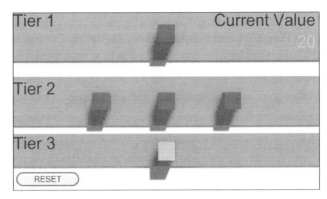

A clearly different from our first test

As you can see, all but one of the child nodes of our root failed, so it reports FAILURE for itself. Let's look at why:

- **Node 2A**: Nothing really changes here from our original example. Our m_currentValue variable starts at 0 and ends up at 10, which is not equal to our m_targetValue of 30, so it fails.

- **Node 2B**: This evaluates its child once more, and because the child node reports SUCCESS, it reports FAILURE for itself, and we move on to the next node.

- **Node 2C**: Once again, we add 10 to our m_currentValue variable, adding up to 20, which, after having changed the m_targetValue variable, no longer evaluates to SUCCESS.

The current implementation of the nodes will have unevaluated nodes default to SUCCESS. This is because of our enum order, as you can see in NodeState.cs:

```
public enum NodeStates {
    SUCCESS,
    FAILURE,
    RUNNING,
}
```

In our enum, SUCCESS is the first enumeration, so if a node never gets evaluated, the default value is never changed. If you were to change the m_targetValue variable to 10, for example, all the nodes would light up to green. This is simply a by-product of our test implementation and doesn't actually reflect any design issues with our nodes. Our UpdateBoxes() method updates all the boxes whether they were evaluated or not. In this example, node 2A would immediately evaluate as SUCCESS, which, in turn, would cause the root node to report SUCCESS, and neither nodes 2B, 2C, nor 3 would be evaluated at all, having no effect on the evaluation of the tree as a whole.

You are highly encouraged to play with this test. Change the root node implementation from a selector to a sequence, for example. By simply changing public Selector m_rootNode; to public Sequence m_rootNode; and m_rootNode = new Selector(rootChildren); to m_rootNode = new Sequence(rootChildren);, you can test a completely different set of functionality.

Summary

In this chapter, we dug in to how a behavior tree works and then we looked at each individual type of node that can make up a behavior tree. We also learned the different scenarios where some nodes would be more helpful than others. After looking at some off-the-shelf solutions available on the Unity asset store, we applied this knowledge by implementing our own basic behavior tree framework in C# and explored the inner workings. With the knowledge and the tools out of the way, we created a sample behavior tree using our framework to test the concepts learned throughout the chapter. This knowledge prepares us to harness the power of behavior trees in games and take our AI implementations to the next level.

In the next chapter, *Chapter 7, Using Fuzzy Logic to Make Your AI Seem Alive*, we'll look at new ways to add complexity and functionality to the concepts we've learned in this chapter, modifying behavior trees, and FSMs, which we covered in *Chapter 2, Finite State Machines and You*, via the concept of fuzzy logic.

7
Using Fuzzy Logic to Make Your AI Seem Alive

Fuzzy logic is a fantastic way to represent the rules of your game in a more nuanced way. Perhaps more so than other concepts in this book, fuzzy logic is a very math-heavy topic. Most of the information can be represented purely in mathematical functions. For the sake of teaching the important concepts as they apply to Unity, most of the math has been simplified and implemented using the Unity's built-in features. Of course, if you are the type who loves math, this is a somewhat deep topic in that regard, so feel free to take the concepts covered in this book and run with them! In this chapter, we'll learn:

- What fuzzy logic is
- Where fuzzy logic is used
- How to implement fuzzy logic controllers
- What the other creative uses for fuzzy logic concepts are

Defining fuzzy logic

The simplest way to define fuzzy logic is by comparison to binary logic. In the previous chapters, we looked at transition rules as true or false or 0 or 1 values. Is something visible? Is it at least a certain distance away? Even in instances where multiple values were being evaluated, all of the values had exactly two outcomes thus, they are binary. In contrast, fuzzy values represent a much richer range of possibilities, where each value is represented as a float rather than an integer. We stop looking at values as 0 or 1, and we start looking at them as 0 to 1.

A common example used to describe fuzzy logic is temperature. Fuzzy logic allows us to make decisions based on non-specific data. I can step outside on a sunny California summer day and ascertain that it is warm, without knowing the temperature precisely. Conversely, if I were to find myself in Alaska during the winter, I would know that it is cold, again, without knowing the exact temperature. These concepts of cold, cool, warm, and hot are fuzzy ones. There is a good amount of ambiguity as to at what point we go from warm to hot. Fuzzy logic allows us to model these concepts as sets and determine their validity or truth by using a set of rules.

When making decisions, people, as it is common to say, has some gray area. That is to say, it's not always black and white. The same concept applies to agents that rely on fuzzy logic. Say you hadn't eaten in a few hours, and you were starting to feel a little hungry. At which point were you hungry enough to go grab a snack? You could look at the time right after a meal as 0, and 1 would be the point where you approached starvation. The following figure illustrates this point:

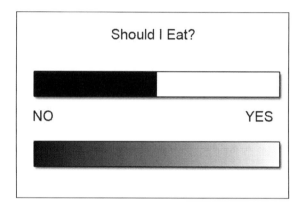

When making decisions, there are many factors that determine the choice. This leads into another aspect of fuzzy logic controllers—they can take into account as much data as necessary. Let's continue to look at our "should I eat?" example. We've only considered one value for making that decision, which is the time since the last time you ate, however, there are other factors that can affect this decision, such as, how much energy you're expending and how lazy you are at that particular moment. Or am I the only one to use that as a deciding factor? Either way, you can see how multiple input values can affect the output, which we can think of as the "likeliness to have another meal".

Fuzzy logic systems can be very flexible due to their generic nature. You provide input, the fuzzy logic provides an output. What that output means to your game is entirely up to you. We've primarily looked at how the inputs would affect a decision, which, in reality, is taking the output and using it in a way the computer, our agent, can understand. However, the output can also be used to determine how much of something to do, or how fast something happens, or for how long something happens. For example, imagine your agent is a car in a sci-fi racing game that has a "nitro-boost" ability that lets it expend a resource to go faster. Our 0 to 1 value can represent a normalized amount of time for it to use that boost or perhaps a normalized amount of fuel to use.

Picking fuzzy systems over binary systems

As with the previous systems we covered in this book, and with most things in game programming, we must evaluate the requirements of our game and the technology and hardware limitations when deciding on the best way to tackle a problem.

As you might imagine, there is a performance cost associated with going from a simple yes/no system to a more nuanced fuzzy logic one, which is one of the reasons we may opt out of using it. Of course, being a more complex system doesn't necessarily always mean it's a better one. There will be times when you just want the simplicity and predictability of a binary system because it may fit your game better.

While there is some truth to the old adage "the simpler, the better", one should also take into account the saying "everything should be made as simple as possible, but not simpler". Though the quote is largely attributed to Albert Einstein, the father of relativity, it's not entirely clear who said it. The important thing to consider is the meaning of the quote itself. You should make your AI as simple as your game needs it to be, but not simpler. Pac-Man's AI works perfectly for the game—it's just simple enough. However, rules say that simple would simply be out of place in a modern shooter or strategy game.

Take the knowledge and examples from this book and find what works best for you.

Using fuzzy logic

Once you understand the simple concepts behind fuzzy logic, it's easy to start thinking of the many, many ways in which it can be useful. In reality, it's just another tool in our belt, and each job requires different tools.

Fuzzy logic is great at taking some data; evaluating it in a way similar to how a human would (albeit in a much simpler way) and then translating the data back to information usable by the system.

Fuzzy logic controllers have several real-world use cases. Some are more obvious than others, and while these are by no means one-to-one comparisons to our usage in game AI, they serve to illustrate a point:

- **Heating ventilation and air conditioning (HVAC) systems**: The temperature example when talking about fuzzy logic is not only a good theoretical approach to explaining fuzzy logic, but also a very common real-world example of fuzzy logic controllers in action.

- **Automobiles**: Modern automobiles come equipped with very sophisticated computerized systems, from the air conditioning system (again) to fuel delivery to automated breaking systems. In fact, putting computers in automobiles has resulted in far more efficient systems than the old binary systems that were sometimes used.

- **Your smartphone**: Ever notice how your screen dims and brightens depending on how much ambient light there is? Modern smartphone operating systems look at ambient light, the color of the data being displayed, and the current battery life to optimize screen brightness.

- **Washing machines**: Not my washing machine necessarily as it's quite old, but most modern washers (from the last 20 years) make some use of fuzzy logic. Load size, water dirtiness, temperature, and other factors are taken into account from cycle to cycle to optimize water use, energy consumption, and time.

If you take a look around your house, there is a good chance you'll find a few interesting uses of fuzzy logic, and I mean besides your computer, of course. While these are "neat" uses of the concept, they're not particularly exciting or game-related. I'm partial to games involving wizards, magic, and monsters, so let's look at a more relevant example.

Implementing a simple fuzzy logic system

For this example, we're going to use my good friend, Bob, the wizard. Bob lives in an RPG world, and he has some very powerful healing magic at his disposal. Bob has to decide when to cast this magic on himself based on his remaining **health points (HPs)**.

In a binary system, Bob's decision-making process might look like this:

```
if(healthPoints <= 50)
{
   CastHealingSpell(me);
}
```

We see that Bob's health can be in one of the two states—above 50 or not. Nothing wrong with that, but let's have a look at what the fuzzy version of this same scenario might look similar to, starting with determining Bob's health status:

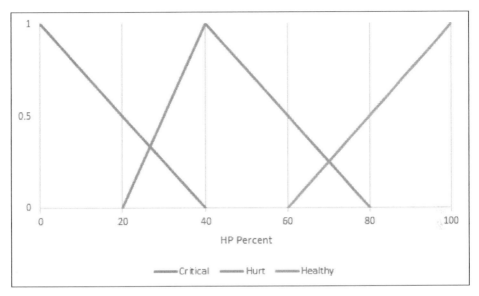

A typical function representing fuzzy values

Before the panic sets in upon seeing charts and values that may not quite mean anything to you right away, let's dissect what we're looking at. Our first impulse might be to try to map the probability that Bob will cast a healing spell to how much health he is missing. That would, in simple terms, just be a linear function. Nothing really fuzzy about that—it's a linear relationship, and while it is a step above a binary decision in terms of complexity, it's still not truly "fuzzy".

Enter the concept of a membership function. It's sort of the key to our system as it allows us to determine how true a statement is. In this example, we're not simply looking at raw values to determine whether or not Bob should cast his spell, but instead we're breaking it up into logical chunks of information for Bob to use in order to determine what his course of action should be.

In this example, we're looking and comparing three statements and evaluating, not only how true each one is, but which is the most true:

- Bob is in critical condition
- Bob is hurt
- Bob is healthy

If you're into official terminology as such, we call this determining the degree of membership to a set. Once we have this information, our agent can determine what to do with it next.

At a glance, you'll notice it's possible for two statements to be true at a time. Bob can be in a critical condition and hurt. He can also be somewhat hurt and a little bit healthy. You're free to pick the thresholds for each, but in this example, let's evaluate these statements as per the preceding graph. The vertical value represents the degree of truth of a statement as a normalized float (0 to 1):

- At 0 percent health, we can see that the critical statement evaluates to 1. It is absolutely true that Bob is critical when his health is gone.
- At 40 percent health, Bob is hurt, and that is the truest statement.
- At 100 percent health, the truest statement is that Bob is healthy.

Anything outside of these absolutely true statements is squarely in fuzzy territory. For example let's say Bob's health is at 65 percent health. In that same chart, we can visualize it like this:

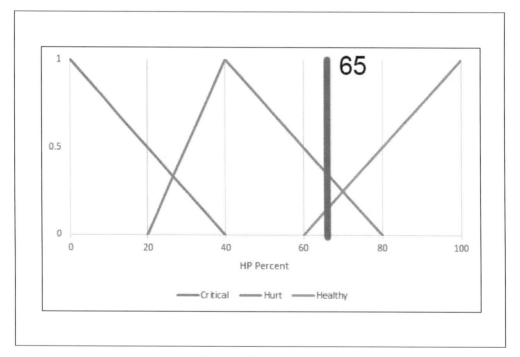

Bob's health at 65 percent

The vertical line drawn through the chart at 65 represents Bob's health. As we can see, it intersects both sets, which means that Bob is a little bit hurt, but he's also kind of healthy. At a glance, we can tell, however, that the vertical line intercepts the "hurt" set at a higher point in the graph. We can take this to mean that Bob is more hurt than he is healthy. To be specific, Bob is 37.5 percent health hurt, 12.5 percent healthy, and 0 percent critical. Let's take a look at this in code; open up our `FuzzySample` scene in Unity. The hierarchy will look like this:

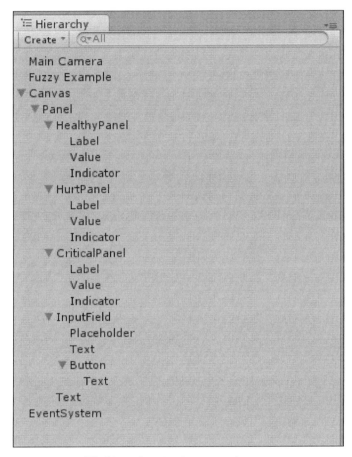

The hierarchy setup in our sample scene

The important game object to look at is `Fuzzy Example`. This contains the logic that we'll be looking at. In addition to that, we have our `Canvas` containing all of the labels and the input field and button that make this example work. Lastly, there's the Unity-generated `EventSystem` and `Camera`, which we can disregard. There isn't anything special going on with the setup for the scene, but it's a good idea to become familiar with it, and you are encouraged to poke around and tweak it to your heart's content after we've looked at why everything is there and what it all does.

With the `Fuzzy Example` game object selected, the inspector will look similar to the following image:

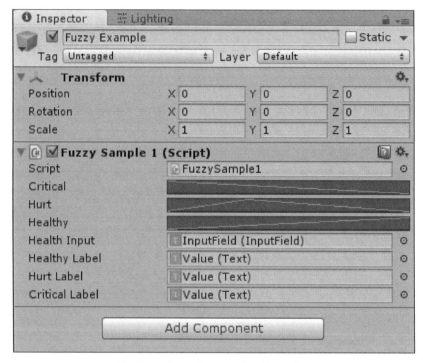

The Fuzzy Example game object inspector

Our sample implementation is not necessarily something you'll take and implement as it is in your game, but it is meant to illustrate the previous points in a clear manner. For the different sets, we use Unity's `AnimationCurve` for each one. It's a quick an easy way to visualize the very same lines in our earlier graph.

Unfortunately, there is no straightforward way to plot all the lines in the same graph, so we use a separate `AnimationCurve` for each set. In the preceding image, they are labeled "Critical", "Hurt", and "Healthy". The neat thing about these curves is that they come with a built-in method to evaluate them at a given point (*t*). For us, *t* does not represent time, but rather the amount of health Bob has.

As in the preceding graph, the Unity example looks at a HP range of 0 to 100. These curves also provide a simple user interface for editing the values. You can simply click on the curve in the inspector. That opens up the curve editing window. You can add points, move points, change tangents, and so on, as shown in the following screenshot:

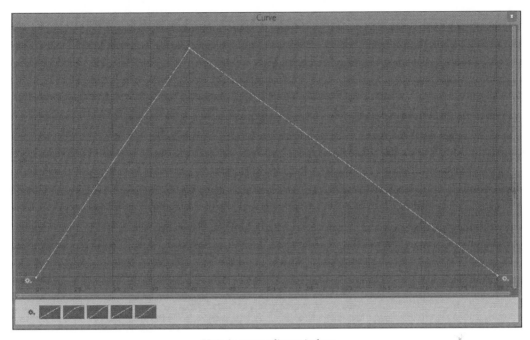

Unity's curve editor window

Our example focuses on triangle-shaped sets. That is, linear graphs for each set. You are by no means restricted to this shape, though it is the most common. You could use a bell curve or a trapezoid for that matter. To keep things simple, we'll stick to the triangle.

 You can learn more about Unity's `AnimationCurve` editor at `http://docs.unity3d.com/ScriptReference/ AnimationCurve.html`.

The rest of the fields are just references to the different UI elements used in code that we'll be looking at later in this chapter. The names of these variables are fairly self-explanatory, however, so there isn't much guesswork to be done here.

Next, we can take a look at how the scene is set up. If you play the scene, the game view will look something similar to the following screenshot:

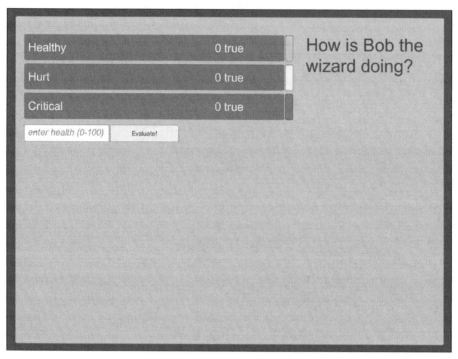

A simple UI to demonstrate fuzzy values

We can see that we have three distinct groups, representing each statement from the Bob the wizard example. How healthy is Bob, how hurt is Bob, and how critical is Bob? For each set, upon evaluating, the value which starts off as "0 true" will dynamically adjust to represent the actual degree of membership.

There is an input box in which you can type a percentage of health to use for the test. No fancy controls are in place for this, so be sure to enter a value from 0 to 100. For the sake of consistency, let's enter a value of 65 into the box and then press the **Evaluate!** button.

This will run some code, look at the curves, and yield the exact same results we saw in our graph earlier. While this shouldn't come as a surprise (the math is what it is, after all), there are fewer things more important in game programming than testing your assumptions, and sure enough, we've tested and verified our earlier statement.

After running the test by hitting the **Evaluate!** button, the game scene will look more similar to the following screenshot:

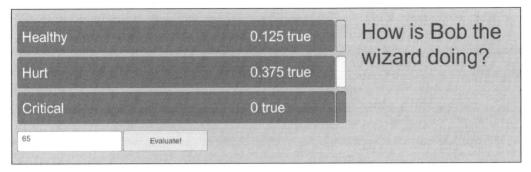

This is how Bob is doing at 65 percent health

Again, the values turn out to be 0.125 (or 12.5 percent) healthy and 0.375 (or 37.5 percent) hurt. At this point, we're still not doing anything with this data, but let's take a look at the code that's handling everything:

```
using UnityEngine;
using UnityEngine.UI;
using System.Collections;

public class FuzzySample1 : MonoBehaviour {
    private const string labelText = "{0} true";
    public AnimationCurve critical;
    public AnimationCurve hurt;
    public AnimationCurve healthy;

    public InputField healthInput;

    public Text healthyLabel;
    public Text hurtLabel;
    public Text criticalLabel;

    private float criticalValue = 0f;
    private float hurtValue = 0f;
    private float healthyValue = 0f;
```

We start off by declaring some variables. The `labelText` is simply a constant we use to plug into our label. We replace the `{0}` with the real value.

Next, we declare the three `AnimationCurve` variables that we mentioned earlier. Making these public or otherwise accessible from the inspector is key to being able to edit them visually (though it is possible to construct curves by code), which is the whole point of using them.

The following four variables are just references to UI elements that we saw earlier in the screenshot of our inspector, and the last three variables are the actual float values that our curves will evaluate into:

```
private void Start () {
    SetLabels();
}


/*
 * Evaluates all the curves and returns float values
 */
public void EvaluateStatements() {
    if (string.IsNullOrEmpty(healthInput.text)) {
        return;
    }
    float inputValue = float.Parse(healthInput.text);

    healthyValue = healthy.Evaluate(inputValue);
    hurtValue = hurt.Evaluate(inputValue);
    criticalValue = critical.Evaluate(inputValue);

    SetLabels();
}
```

The `Start()` method doesn't require much explanation. We simply update our labels here so that they initialize to something other than the default text. The `EvaluateStatements()` method is much more interesting. We first do some simple null checking for our input string. We don't want to try and parse an empty string, so we return out of the function if it is empty. As mentioned earlier, there is no check in place to validate that you've input a numerical value, so be sure not to accidentally input a non-numerical value or you'll get an error.

For each of the `AnimationCurve` variables, we call the `Evaluate(float t)` method, where we replace `t` with the parsed value we get from the input field. In the example we ran, that value would be 65. Then, we update our labels once again to display the values we got. The code looks similar to this:

```
/*
 * Updates the GUI with the evaluated values based
 * on the health percentage entered by the
```

```
    * user.
    */
    private void SetLabels() {
        healthyLabel.text = string.Format(labelText, healthyValue);
        hurtLabel.text = string.Format(labelText, hurtValue);
        criticalLabel.text = string.Format(labelText, criticalValue);
    }
}
```

We simply take each label and replace the text with a formatted version of our
labelText constant that replaces the {0} with the real value.

Expanding the sets

We discussed this topic in detail earlier, and it's important to understand that
the values that make up the sets in our example are unique to Bob and his pain
threshold. Let's say we have a second wizard, Jim, who's a bit more reckless. For him,
"critical" might be below 20 rather than 40, as it is for Bob. This is what I like to call
a "happy bonus" from using fuzzy logic. Each agent in the game can have different
rules that define their sets, but the system doesn't care. You could predefine these
rules or have some degree or randomness determine the limits, and every single
agent would behave uniquely and respond to things in their own way.

In addition, there is no reason to limit our sets to just three. Why not four or five? To
the fuzzy logic controller, all that matters is that you determine what truth you're
trying to arrive at, and how you get there; it doesn't care how many different sets or
possibilities exist in that system.

Defuzzifying the data

Yes, that's a real (sort of) word. We've started with some crisp rules, which, in the
context of fuzzy logic, means clear-cut, hard-defined data, which we then fuzzified
(again, a sort of real word) by assigning membership functions to sets. The last step
of the process is to defuzzify the data and make a decision. For this, we use simple
Boolean operations, that is:

```
IF health IS critical THEN cast healing spell
```

Now, at this point, you may be saying, "Hold on a second. That looks an awful lot
like a binary controller," and you'd be correct. So why go through all the trouble?
Remember what we said earlier about ambiguous information? Without a fuzzy
controller, how does our agent understand what it means to be critical, hurt, or
healthy for that matter? These are abstract concepts that mean very little on their
own to a computer.

By using fuzzy logic, we're now able to use these vague terms, infer something from them, and do concrete things; in this case, cast a healing spell. Furthermore, we're able to allow each agent to determine what these vague terms mean to them at an individual level, allowing us not only to achieve unpredictability at an individual level, but even amongst several similar agents.

The process is described best in the following diagram:

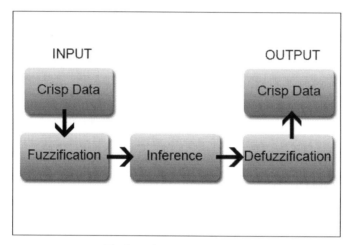

The fuzzy logic controller flow

At the end of the day, they are still computers, so we're bound to the most basic thing computers understand: 0s and 1s:

- We start with, crisp data, that is, concrete, hard values that tell us something very specific.

- The fuzzification step is where we get to decide the abstract or ambiguous data that our agent will need to make a decision.

- During the inference step, our agent gets to decide what that data means. The agent gets to determine what is "true" based on a provided set of rules, meant to mimic the nuance of human decision-making.

- The defuzzification step takes this human-friendly data and converts it into simple computer-friendly information.

- We end with crisp data, ready for our wizard agent to use.

Using the resulting crisp data

The data output from a fuzzy controller can then be plugged into a behavior tree or a finite state machine. Of course, we can also combine multiple controllers' output to make decisions. In fact, we can take a whole bunch of them to achieve the most realistic or interesting result (as convincing as a magic-using wizard can be, anyway). The following figure illustrates a potential set of fuzzy logic controllers it can use to determine whether or not to cast the heal spell:

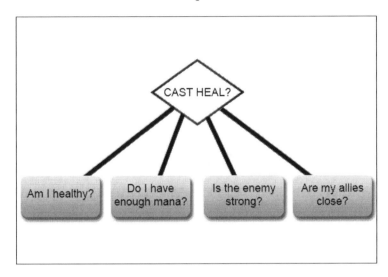

We've looked at the health question already, but what about the rest? We have another set of questions that really don't mean much to our agent on their own:

Do you have enough mana? Well, you can have a little bit of mana, some mana, or a lot of mana. It would not be uncommon for a human player to ask this question as they choose to cast a magic spell in a game or use an ability. "Enough" may literally be a binary amount, but more likely, it would be "enough to cast heal, and have some left for other spells". We start with a straightforward crisp value—the amount of mana the agent has available that we then stick to our fuzzy logic controller and get some crisp data at the other end.

What about the enemy's strength? He could be weak, average, strong, or unbeatable. You can get creative with the input for your fuzzy logic controllers. You could, for example, just take a raw "strength" value from your enemy, but you could also take the difference between your "defensive" stat and the enemy's "attack power", and plug that into your fuzzy logic controller. Remember, there is no restriction on how you process the data before it goes into the controller.

Are my allies close? As we saw in *Chapter 2, Finite State Machines and You*, a simple distance check can do wonders for a simple design, but at times, you may need more than just that. You may need to take into account obstacles along the way — is that an ally behind a locked gate, making him unable to reach the agent? These types of questions could even be a nested set of statements that we need to evaluate.

Now, if we were to take that last question with the nested controllers, it might start to look a little familiar.

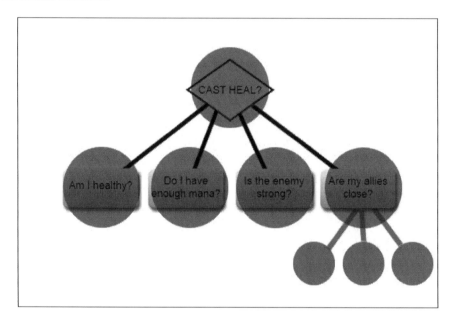

The preceding figure is quite tree-like, isn't it? Sure enough, there is no reason why you couldn't build a behavior tree using fuzzy logic to evaluate each node. We end up with a very flexible, powerful, and nuanced AI system by combining these two concepts.

Using a simpler approach

If you choose to stick with a simple evaluation of the crisp output, in other words, not specifically a tree or an FSM, you can use more Boolean operators to decide what your agent is going to do. The pseudo code would look like this:

```
IF health IS critical AND mana IS plenty THEN cast heal
```

We can check for conditions that are not true:

```
IF health IS critical AND allies ARE NOT close THEN cast heal
```

And we can also string multiple conditions together:

```
IF health IS critical AND mana IS NOT depleted AND enemy IS very
strong THEN cast heal
```

By looking at these simplified statements, you have noticed yet another "happy bonus" of using fuzzy logic—the crisp output abstracts much of the decision-making conditionals and combines them into simplified data.

Rather than having to parse through all the possibilities in your `if/else` statements and ending up with a bazillion of them or a gazillion switch statements, you can neatly bundle pockets of logic into fewer, more meaningful chunks of data.

In other words, you don't have to nest all the statements in a procedural way that is hard to read and difficult to reuse. As a design pattern, abstracting data via a fuzzy logic controller ends up being much more object-oriented and friendlier.

Finding other uses for fuzzy logic

Fuzzy data is very peculiar and interesting in that it can be used in tandem with all of the major concepts we introduced in this book. We saw how a series of fuzzy logic controllers can easily fit into a behavior tree structure, and it's not terribly difficult to imagine how it can be used with an FSM.

Merging with other concepts

Sensory systems also tend to make use of fuzzy logic. While seeing something can be a binary condition, in low-light or low-contrast environments, we can suddenly see how fuzzy the condition can become. You've probably experienced it at night— seeing an odd shape, dark in the distance, in the shadows, thinking "is that a cat?" which then turns out to be a trash bag, some other animal, or perhaps even your imagination. The same can be applied to sounds and smells.

When it comes to pathfinding, we run into the cost of traversing certain areas of a grid, which, a fuzzy logic controller can easily help fuzzify and make more interesting.

Should Bob cross the bridge and fight his way through the guards or risk crossing the river and fighting the current? Well, if he's a good swimmer and a poor fighter, the choice is clear, right?

Creating a truly unique experience

Our agents can use fuzzy logic to mimic personalities. Some agents may be more "brave" than others. Suddenly, their personal characteristics—how fast they are, how far they can run, their size, and so on, can be leveraged to arrive at the decisions that are unique to that agent.

Personalities can be applied to enemies, allies, friends, NPCs, or even to the rules of the game. The game can take in crisp data from the player's progress, style of play, or level of progression, and dynamically adjust the difficulty to provide a more unique and personalized challenge.

Fuzzy logic can even be used to dole out the technical game rules, such as number of players in a given multiplayer lobby, the type of data to display to the player, and even how players are matched against other players. Taking the player's statistics and plugging those into a matchmaking system can help keep the player engaged by pitting him against the players that either match his style of play in a cooperative environment or players of similar skill level in a competitive environment.

Summary

Glad to see that you've made it to the end of the chapter. Fuzzy logic tends to become far less fuzzy once you understand the basic concepts. Being one of the more math-pure concepts in the book, it can be a little daunting if you're not familiar with the lingo, but when presented in a familiar context, the mystery fades away, and you're left with a very powerful tool to use in your game.

We learned how fuzzy logic is used in the real world, and how it can help illustrate vague concepts in a way that binary systems cannot. We also learned how to implement our own fuzzy logic controllers using the concepts of member functions, degrees of membership, and fuzzy sets. Lastly, we explored the various ways in which we can use the resulting data, and how it can help make our agents more unique.

In the final chapter, we will look at several of the concepts introduced in the book working together.

8
How It All Comes Together

We've almost arrived at the end of our journey. We learned all the essential tools to implement fun AI in our Unity game. We stressed on this throughout the course of the book, but it's important to drive the point home: the concepts and patterns we learned throughout the book are individual concepts, but they can, and often should, be used in harmony to achieve the desired behavior from our AI. Before we say our goodbyes, we'll look at a simple tank-defense game that implements some of the concepts that we learned to achieve a cohesive "game", and I only say "game" because this is more of a blueprint for you to expand upon and play with. In this chapter, we will:

- Integrate some of the systems we've learned in a single project
- Create an AI tower agent
- Create our `NavMeshAgent` tank
- Set up the environment
- Test our sample scene

Setting up the rules

Our "game" is quite simple. While the actual game logic, such as health, damage, and win conditions, are left completely up to you, our example focuses on setting you up to implement your own tank-defense game.

When deciding on what kind of logic and behavior you'll need from your agent, it's important to have the rules of the game fleshed out beyond a simple idea. Of course, as you implement different features, those rules can change, but having a set of concepts nailed down early on will help you pick the best tools for the job.

It's a bit of a twist on the traditional tower-defense genre. You don't build towers to stop an oncoming enemy; you rather use your abilities to help your tank get through a gauntlet of towers. As your tank traverses the maze, towers along the path will attempt to destroy your tank by shooting explosive projectiles at it. To help your tank get to the other side, you can use two abilities:

- **Boost**: This ability doubles up your tank's movement speed for a short period of time. This is great for getting away from a projectile in a bind.

- **Shield**: This creates a shield around your tank for a short period of time to block oncoming projectiles.

For our example, we'll implement the towers using a finite state machine since they have a limited number of states and don't require the extra complexity of a behavior tree. The towers will also need to be able to be aware of their surroundings, or more specifically, whether the tank is nearby so that they can shoot at it, so we'll use a sphere trigger to model the towers' field of vision and sensing. The tank needs to be able to navigate the environment on its own, so we use a NavMesh and `NavMeshAgent` to achieve this.

Creating the towers

In the sample project for this chapter, you'll find a `Tower` prefab in the `Prefabs` folder. The tower itself is quite simple; it's just a group of primitives arranged to look like a cannon, as you can see in the following screenshot:

Our beautiful primitive shape tower

The barrel of the gun is affixed to the spherical part of the tower. The gun can rotate freely on its axis when tracking the player so that it can fire in the direction of its target, but it is immobile in any other way. Once the tank gets far enough away, the tower cannot chase it or reposition itself.

In the sample scene, there are several towers placed throughout the level. As they are prefabbed, it's very easy to duplicate towers, move them around, and reuse them between the levels. Their setup is not terribly complicated either. Their hierarchy looks similar to the following screenshot:

The Tower hierarchy in the inspector

The breakdown of the hierarchy is as follows:

- `Tower`: Technically, this is the base of the tower — the cylinder that holds the rest of it up. This serves no function but to hold the rest of the parts.

- `Gun`: The gun is where most of the magic happens. It is the sphere mounted on the tower with the barrel on it. This is the part of the tower that moves and tracks the player.

- `Barrel` and `Muzzle`: The muzzle is located at the tip of the barrel. This is used as the spawn point for the bullets that come out of the gun.

We mentioned that the gun is where the business happens for the tower, so let's dig in a bit deeper. The inspector with the gun selected looks similar to the following screenshot:

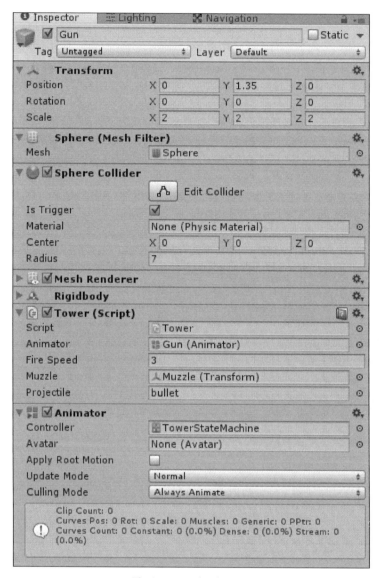

The inspector for the gun

There is quite a bit going on in the inspector here. Let's look at each of the components that affect the logic:

- **Sphere Collider**: This is essentially the tower's range. When the tank enters this sphere, the tower can detect it and will lock on to it to begin shooting at it. This is our implementation of perception for the tower. Notice that the radius is set to 7. The value can be changed to whatever you liked, but 7 seems to be a fair value. Also, note that we set the **Is Trigger** checkbox to true. We don't want this sphere to actually cause collisions, just to fire trigger events.

- **Rigidbody**: This component is required for the collider to actually work properly whether objects are moving or not. This is because Unity does not send collision or trigger events to game objects that are not moving, unless they have a rigid body component.

- **Tower**: This is the logic script for the tower. It works in tandem with the state machine and the state machine behavior, but we'll look at these components more in depth shortly.

- **Animator**: This is our tower's state machine. It doesn't actually handle animation.

Before we look at the code that drives the tower, let's take a brief look at the state machine. It's not terribly complicated, as you can see in the following screenshot:

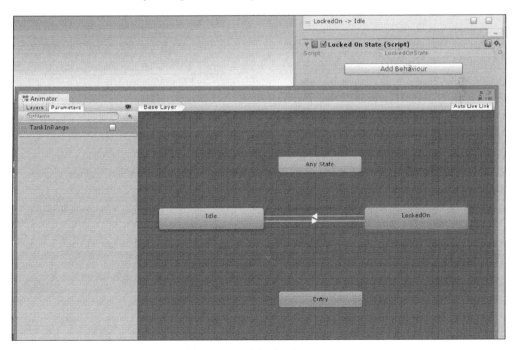

The state machine for the tower

There are two states that we care about: Idle (the default state) and LockedOn. The transition from Idle to LockedOn happens when the TankInRange bool is set to true, and the reverse transition happens when the bool is set to false.

The LockedOn state has a StateMachineBehaviour class attached to it, which we'll look at next:

```
using UnityEngine;
using System.Collections;

public class LockedOnState : StateMachineBehaviour {

    GameObject player;
    Tower tower;

    // OnStateEnter is called when a transition starts and the state
    machine starts to evaluate this state
    override public void OnStateEnter(Animator animator,
    AnimatorStateInfo stateInfo, int layerIndex) {
        player = GameObject.FindWithTag("Player");
        tower = animator.gameObject.GetComponent<Tower>();
        tower.LockedOn = true;
    }


    //OnStateUpdate is called on each Update frame between
    OnStateEnter and OnStateExit callbacks
    override public void OnStateUpdate(Animator animator,
    AnimatorStateInfo stateInfo, int layerIndex) {
        animator.gameObject.transform.LookAt(player.transform);
    }

    // OnStateExit is called when a transition ends and the state
    machine finishes evaluating this state
    override public void OnStateExit(Animator animator,
    AnimatorStateInfo stateInfo, int layerIndex) {
        animator.gameObject.transform.rotation = Quaternion.identity;
        tower.LockedOn = false;
    }
}
```

When we enter the state and OnStateEnter is called, we find a reference to our player. In the provided example, the player is tagged as "Player" so that we are able to get a reference to it using GameObject.FindWithTag. Next, we fetch a reference to the Tower component attached to our tower prefab and set its LockedOn bool to true.

As long as we're in the state, OnStateUpdate gets called on each frame. Inside this method, we get a reference to the Gun GameObject (which the Tower component is attached to) via the provided Animator reference. We use this reference to the gun to have it track the tank using Transform.LookAt.

 Alternatively, as the LockedOn bool of the Tower is set to true, this logic could be handled in the Tower.cs script, instead.

Lastly, as we exit the state, OnStateExit gets called. We use this method to do a little cleanup. We reset the rotation of our gun to indicate that it is no longer tracking the player, and we set the Tower's LockedOn bool back to false.

As we can see, this StateMachineBehaviour interacts with the Tower.cs script, so let's look at Tower.cs next for a bit more context as to what's happening:

```
using UnityEngine;
using System.Collections;

public class Tower : MonoBehaviour {
    [SerializeField]
    private Animator animator;

    [SerializeField]
    private float fireSpeed = 3f;
    private float fireCounter = 0f;
    private bool canFire = true;

    [SerializeField]
    private Transform muzzle;
    [SerializeField]
    private GameObject projectile;

    private bool isLockedOn = false;

    public bool LockedOn {
        get { return isLockedOn; }
        set { isLockedOn = value; }
    }
}
```

First up, we declare our variables and properties.

We need a reference to our state machine; this is where the Animator variable comes in. The next three variables, fireSpeed, fireCounter, and canFire all relate to our tower's shooting logic. We'll see how that works up later.

As we mentioned earlier, the muzzle is the location the bullets will spawn from when shooting. The projectile is the prefab we're going to instantiate.

Lastly, isLockedOn is get and set via LockedOn. While this book, in general, strays away from enforcing any particular coding convention, it's generally a good idea to keep values private unless explicitly required to be public, so instead of making isLockedOn public, we provide a property for it to access it remotely (in this case, from the LockedOnSate behavior):

```
private void Update() {
        if (LockedOn && canFire) {
            StartCoroutine(Fire());
        }
    }


    private void OnTriggerEnter(Collider other) {
        if (other.tag == "Player") {
            animator.SetBool("TankInRange", true);
        }
    }


    private void OnTriggerExit(Collider other) {
        if (other.tag == "Player") {
            animator.SetBool("TankInRange", false);
        }
    }


    private void FireProjectile() {
        GameObject bullet = Instantiate(projectile, muzzle.position,
muzzle.rotation) as GameObject;
        bullet.GetComponent<Rigidbody>().AddForce(muzzle.forward *
300);
    }


    private IEnumerator Fire() {
        canFire = false;
```

```
        FireProjectile();
        while (fireCounter < fireSpeed) {
            fireCounter += Time.deltaTime;
            yield return null;
        }
        canFire = true;
        fireCounter = 0f;
    }
}
```

Next up, we have all our methods, and the meat and potatoes of the tower logic. Inside the `Update` loop, we check for two things: are we locked on and can we fire? If both are true, we fire off our `Fire()` coroutine. We'll look at why `Fire()` is a coroutine before coming back to the `OnTrigger` messages.

 Coroutines can be a tricky concept to grasp if you're not already familiar with them. For more information on how to use them, check out Unity's documentation at `http://docs.unity3d.com/Manual/Coroutines.html`.

As we don't want our tower to be able to constantly shoot projectiles at the tank like a projectile-crazy death machine, we use the variables that we defined earlier to create a cushion between each shot. After we call `FireProjectile()` and set `canFire` to `false`, we start a counter from 0 up to `fireSpeed`, before we set `canFire` to `true` again. The `FireProjectile()` method handles the instantiation of the projectile and shoots it out toward the direction the gun is pointing to using `Rigidbody.AddForce`. The actual bullet logic is handled elsewhere, but we'll look at that later.

Lastly, we have our two `OnTrigger` events — one for when something enters the trigger attached to this component and another for when an object leaves said trigger. Remember the `TankInRange` bool that drives the transitions for our state machine? This variable gets set to `true` here when we enter the trigger and back to `false` as we exit. Essentially, when the tank enters the gun's sphere of "vision", it instantly locks on to the tank, and the lock is released when the tank leaves the sphere.

Making the towers shoot

If we look back at our Tower component in the inspector, you'll notice that a prefab named bullet is assigned to the projectile variable. This prefab can be found in the Prefabs folder of the sample project. The prefab looks similar to the following screenshot:

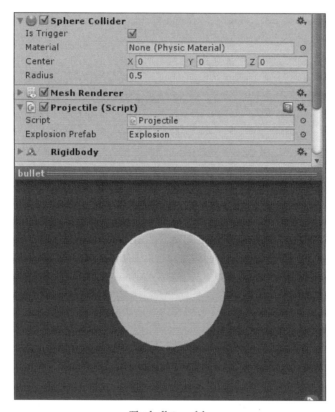

The bullet prefab

The bullet game object is nothing fancy; it's just a bright yellow orb. There is a sphere collider attached to it, and once again, we must make sure that IsTrigger is set to true and it has a Rigidbody (with gravity turned off) attached to it. We also have a Projectile component attached to the bullet prefab. This handles the collision logic. Let's take a look at the code:

```
using UnityEngine;
using System.Collections;

public class Projectile : MonoBehaviour {

    [SerializeField]
```

```
    private GameObject explosionPrefab;

  void Start () {   }

    private void OnTriggerEnter(Collider other) {
        if (other.tag == "Player" || other.tag == "Environment") {
            if (explosionPrefab == null) {
                return;
            }
            GameObject explosion = Instantiate(explosionPrefab,
transform.position, Quaternion.identity) as GameObject;
            Destroy(this.gameObject);
        }
    }
}
```

We have a fairly straightforward script here. In our level, we have all of the floor and walls tagged as "Environment", so in our OnTriggerEnter method, we check that the trigger this projectile is colliding with is either the player or the environment. If it is, we instantiate an explosion prefab and destroy the projectile. Let's take a look at the explosion prefab, which looks similar to this:

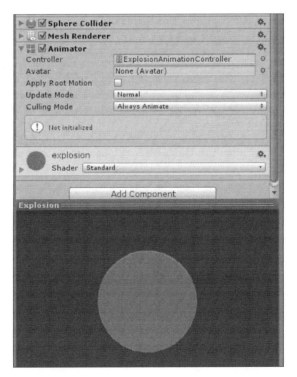

Inspector with the explosion prefab selected

As we can see, there is a very similar game object here; we have a sphere collider with `IsTrigger` set to `true`. The main difference is an `animator` component. When this `explosion` is instantiated, it expands as an explosion would, then we use the state machine to destroy the instance when it transitions out of its explosion state. The `animation` controller looks similar to the following screenshot:

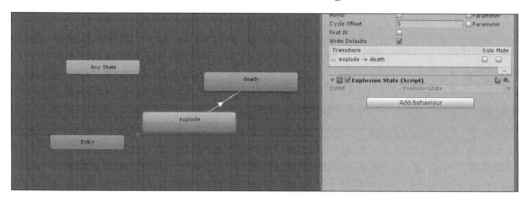

The animation controller driving the explosion prefab

You'll notice the `explode` state has a behavior attached to it. The code inside this behavior is fairly simple:

```
// OnStateExit is called when a transition ends and the state machine
finishes evaluating this state
    override public void OnStateExit(Animator animator,
AnimatorStateInfo stateInfo, int layerIndex) {
        Destroy(animator.gameObject, 0.1f);
    }
```

All we're doing here is destroying the instance of the object when we exit the state, which occurs when the animation ends.

 If you want to flesh out the game with your own game logic, this may be a good place to trigger any secondary effects such as damage, environment particles, or anything you can think of!

Setting up the tank

The example project also includes a prefab for the tank, which is simply called (you guessed it) `Tank`, inside the `Prefabs` folder.

The tank itself is a simple agent with one goal—reach the end of the maze. As mentioned earlier, the player has to help the tank out along the way by activating its abilities to keep it safe from oncoming fire from the towers.

By now you should be fairly familiar with the components you'll encounter along the way, except for the `Tank.cs` component attached to the prefab. Let's take a look at the code to figure out what's going on behind the scenes:

```
using UnityEngine;
using System.Collections;

public class Tank : MonoBehaviour {
    [SerializeField]
    private Transform goal;
    private NavMeshAgent agent;
    [SerializeField]
    private float speedBoostDuration = 3;
    [SerializeField]
    private ParticleSystem boostParticleSystem;
    [SerializeField]
    private float shieldDuration = 3f;
    [SerializeField]
    private GameObject shield;

    private float regularSpeed = 3.5f;
    private float boostedSpeed = 7.0f;
    private bool canBoost = true;
    private bool canShield = true;
```

There are a number of values that we want to be able to tweak easily, so we declare the corresponding variables first. Everything from the duration of our abilities to the effects associated with them is set here first:

```
    private bool hasShield = false;
    private void Start() {
        agent = GetComponent<NavMeshAgent>();
        agent.SetDestination(goal.position);
    }

    private void Update() {
        if (Input.GetKeyDown(KeyCode.B)) {
            if (canBoost) {
                StartCoroutine(Boost());
            }
        }
        if (Input.GetKeyDown(KeyCode.S)) {
            if (canShield) {
                StartCoroutine(Shield());
            }
        }
    }
```

Our `Start` method simply does some setup for our tank; it grabs the `NavMeshAgent` component and sets its destination to be equal to our goal variable. We will discuss more on that soon.

We use the `Update` method to catch the input for our abilities. We've mapped `B` to `boost` and `S` to `shield`. As these are timed abilities, much like the towers' ability to shoot, we implement these via coroutines:

```
private IEnumerator Shield() {
        canShield = false;
        shield.SetActive(true);
        float shieldCounter = 0f;
        while (shieldCounter < shieldDuration) {
            shieldCounter += Time.deltaTime;
            yield return null;
        }
        canShield = true;
        shield.SetActive(false);
}

private IEnumerator Boost() {
        canBoost = false;
        agent.speed = boostedSpeed;
        boostParticleSystem.Play();
        float boostCounter = 0f;
        while (boostCounter < speedBoostDuration) {
            boostCounter += Time.deltaTime;
            yield return null;
        }
        canBoost = true;
        boostParticleSystem.Pause();
        agent.speed = regularSpeed;
}
```

The two abilities' logic is very similar. The `shield` enables and disables the `shield` game object, which we define in a variable in the inspector, and after an amount of time equal to `shieldDuration` has passed, we turn it off, and allow the player to use the `shield` again.

The main difference in the `Boost` code is that rather than enabling and disabling a game object, the `boost` calls `Play` on a particle system we assign via the inspector and also sets the speed of our `NavMeshAgent` to double the original value, before resetting it at the end of the ability's duration.

Can you think of other abilities you'd give the tank? This is a very straightforward pattern that you can use to implement new abilities in your own variant of the project. You can also add additional logic to customize the shield and boost abilities here.

The sample scene already has an instance of the tank in it with all the variables properly set up. The inspector for the tank in the sample scene looks similar to the following screenshot:

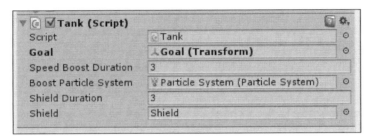

Inspector with the tank instance selected

As you can see in the preceding screenshot, we've assigned the `Goal` variable to a transform with the same name, which is located in the scene at the end of the maze we've set up. We can also tweak the duration of our abilities here, which is set to **3** by default. You can also swap out the art for the abilities, be it the particle system used in the boost or the game object used for the shield.

The last bit of code to look at is the code driving the camera. We want the camera to follow the player, but only along its z value, horizontally down the track. The code to achieve this looks similar to this:

```
using UnityEngine;
using System.Collections;

public class HorizontalCam : MonoBehaviour {
    [SerializeField]
    private Transform target;

    private Vector3 targetPositon;

    private void Update() {
        targetPositon = transform.position;
        targetPositon.z = target.transform.position.z;
        transform.position = Vector3.Lerp(transform.position,
targetPositon, Time.deltaTime);
    }
}
```

As you can see, we simply set the target position of the camera equal to its current position on all axes, but we then assign the *z* axis of the target position to be the same as our target's, which if you look in the inspector, has been set to the transform of the tank. We then use linear interpolation (`Vector3.Lerp`) to smoothly translate the camera from its current position to its target position every frame.

Setting up the environment

As our tank uses a `NavMeshAgent` component to traverse the environment, we need to set up our scene using static game objects for the bake process to work properly, as we learned in *Chapter 4, Finding Your Way*. The maze is set up in a way so that towers are spread out fairly reasonably and that the tank has plenty of space to maneuver around easily. The following screenshot shows the general layout of the maze:

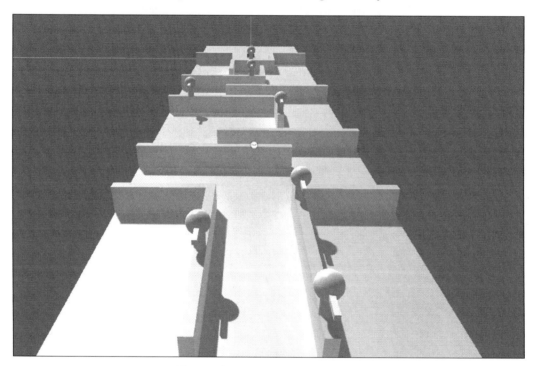

The gauntlet our tank must run through

As you can see, there are seven towers spread out through the maze and a few twists and turn for our tank to break line of sight. In order to avoid having our tank graze the walls, we adjust the settings in the navigation window to our liking. By default, the example scene has the agent radius set to 1.46 and the step height to 1.6. There are no hard rules for how we arrived at these numbers; it is just trial and error.

After baking the NavMesh, we'll end up with something similar to what's shown in the following screenshot:

The scene after we've baked our NavMesh

Feel free to rearrange the walls and towers to your liking. Just remember that any blocking objects you add to the scene must be marked as static, and you have to rebake the navigation for the scene after you've set everything up just the way you like it.

Testing the example

The example scene is ready to play right out of the box, so if you didn't get the itch to modify any of the default settings, you can just hit the **Play** button and watch your tank go. You'll notice we've added a canvas with a label explaining the controls to the player. There is nothing fancy going on here; it's just a simple "press this button to do that" kind of instruction:

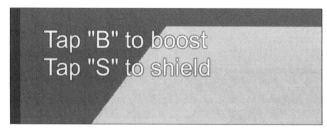

Simple instructions to guide the player

The example project is a great example to expand upon and to have fun with. With the concepts learned throughout this book, you can expand on the types of towers, the tank's abilities, the rules, or even give the tank a more complex, nuanced behavior. For now, we can see that the concepts of state machines, navigation, perception and sensing, and steering, all come together in a simple, yet amusing example. The following screenshot shows the game in action:

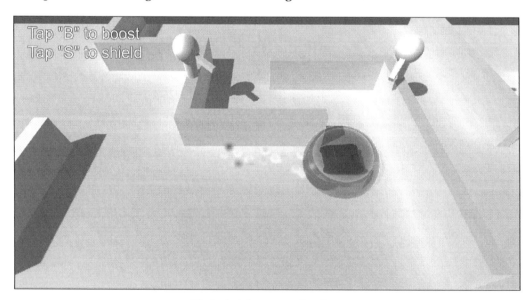

The tank-defense game in action

Summary

So, we've reached the end. In this chapter, we took a few of the concepts covered in the book and applied them to create a small tank-defense game. We built upon the concept of finite state machines, which we originally covered in *Chapter 2, Finite State Machines and You*, and created an artificial intelligence to drive our enemy towers' behavior. We then enhanced the behavior by combining it with sensing and perception, and finally, we implemented navigation via Unity's NavMesh feature to help our tank AI navigate through our maze-like level, through a gauntlet of autonomous AI towers with one thing on their simple AI minds—destroy!

Index

Thank you for buying
Unity AI Game Programming
Second Edition

About Packt Publishing

Packt, pronounced 'packed', published its first book, *Mastering phpMyAdmin for Effective MySQL Management*, in April 2004, and subsequently continued to specialize in publishing highly focused books on specific technologies and solutions.

Our books and publications share the experiences of your fellow IT professionals in adapting and customizing today's systems, applications, and frameworks. Our solution-based books give you the knowledge and power to customize the software and technologies you're using to get the job done. Packt books are more specific and less general than the IT books you have seen in the past. Our unique business model allows us to bring you more focused information, giving you more of what you need to know, and less of what you don't.

Packt is a modern yet unique publishing company that focuses on producing quality, cutting-edge books for communities of developers, administrators, and newbies alike. For more information, please visit our website at www.packtpub.com.

Writing for Packt

We welcome all inquiries from people who are interested in authoring. Book proposals should be sent to author@packtpub.com. If your book idea is still at an early stage and you would like to discuss it first before writing a formal book proposal, then please contact us; one of our commissioning editors will get in touch with you.

We're not just looking for published authors; if you have strong technical skills but no writing experience, our experienced editors can help you develop a writing career, or simply get some additional reward for your expertise.

Getting Started with Unity 5

ISBN: 978-1-78439-831-6   Paperback: 184 pages

Leverage the power of Unity 5 to create amazing 3D games

1. Learn to create interactive games with the Unity 5 game engine.

2. Explore advanced features of Unity 5 to help make your games more appealing and successful.

3. A step-by-step guide giving you the perfect start to developing games with Unity 5.

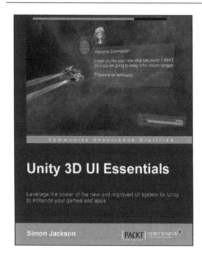

Unity 3D UI Essentials

ISBN: 978-1-78355-361-7   Paperback: 280 pages

Leverage the power of the new and improved UI system for Unity to enhance your games and apps

1. Discover how to build efficient UI layouts coping with multiple resolutions and screen sizes.

2. In-depth overview of all the new UI features that give you creative freedom to drive your game development to new heights.

3. Walk through many different examples of UI layout from simple 2D overlays to in-game 3D implementations.

Please check **www.PacktPub.com** for information on our titles

PUBLISHING

Unity 4.x Game AI Programming

ISBN: 978-1-84969-340-0   Paperback: 232 pages

Learn and implement game AI in Unity3D with a lot of sample projects and next-generation techniques to use in your Unity3D projects

1. A practical guide with step-by-step instructions and example projects to learn Unity3D scripting.

2. Learn pathfinding using A* algorithms as well as Unity3D pro features and navigation graphs.

3. Implement finite state machines (FSMs), path following, and steering algorithms.

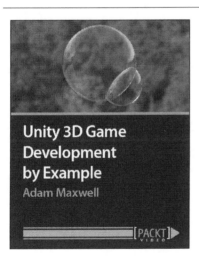

Unity 3D Game Development by Example [Video]

ISBN: 978-1-84969-530-5   Duration: 02:30 hours

Learn how Unity3D "Thinks" by understanding Unity's UI and project structure to start building fun games in Unity3D right away

1. Two and a half hours of Unity screencast tutorials, broken into bite-sized sections.

2. Create 3D graphics, sound, and challenging gameplay.

3. Build game UI, high score tables, and other extra features.

4. Program powerful game logic with C# scripting.

Please check **www.PacktPub.com** for information on our titles